Robert Winkler Burke, of Reno, NV, studied evangelical Christianity to see differences between existent immaturity and the hope of maturity. He discovered maturity has its own higher language and surprising outcome. He says his work is a magnum opus/Rosetta Stone...a sword like no other.

Robert Winkler Burke

THINK! LIKE AN ADVANCED CHRISTIAN

AUSTIN MACAULEY PUBLISHERS™

LONDON • CAMBRIDGE • NEW YORK • SHARJAH

Ordering Information
Quantity sales: Special discounts are available on quantity purchases by corporations, associations, and others. For details, contact the publisher at the address below.

Publisher's Cataloging-in-Publication data
Burke, Robert Winkler
Think! Like an Advanced Christian

ISBN 9781645362036 (Paperback)
ISBN 9781645362029 (Hardback)
ISBN 9781645368465 (ePub e-book)

Library of Congress Control Number: 2020908367

www.austinmacauley.com/us

First Published (2021)
Austin Macauley Publishers LLC
40 Wall Street, 33rd Floor, Suite 3302
New York, NY 10005
USA

mail-usa@austinmacauley.com
+1 (646) 5125767

Thanks to my dad and mom, Ray and Jimmye Burke, for their ever-lasting support.

Thanks also to Kenyan pastor, Benjamin Wamalwa Khaemba, and cousin Sharon Tomme for spiritual support.

Thanks to Russian Martial Art Systema's Vladimir Vasiliev and Mikhail Ryabko.

Table of Contents

(As one thinks, one is, so think well!)
(What you do, has its way with you!)
*(The God mystery is: **Christ-in-You!**)*

Jeremiah 6:16—Thus says the LORD, "Stand by the ways and see and ask for the ancient paths, Where the good way is, and walk in it; And you will find rest for your souls. But they said, 'We will not walk in it.'"—New American Standard Bible

Caution:

Ezekiel 5:15 says: *"<u>I shall execute judgments in thee in anger and in fury and in furious rebukes. I the Lord have spoken it</u>." The Lord's fury includes caricatures that are exaggerations by means of ludicrous distortion, burlesque mockery, and earthy expressions that shock and reduce religious intellectualisms to the common truths of the common man. For a common man sees and says when a king has no clothes, despite the royal retinue's protestations that nothing obscene is happening but for that foul commoner who dares accuse (gasp!) their royal entourage of being stark, hideous, stupid naked.*

<u>Note from Robert Winkler Burke regarding any claims of inerrancy</u>: The Lord's work speaks for itself and the Lord Himself speaks for Himself in this body of work. However, you would be doing me a great favor, indeed, to agree with me that I am not perfect. However, I hope that even though mistakes can herein be found—*like Moses who struck the rock in disobedience (or the Egyptian), or like John the Baptist who questioned Christ's identity from his prison cell, or Elijah who ran from Jezebel, or John the Revelator who worshipped before the feet of an angel (and that on the last page of the Bible!)*—I pray you believe such

10

fallible humans are not altogether despicable in their efforts to provide a body of work for the body of Christ. All who manifest God, manifest Him differently. This we must honor, despite urges to stone them first as an act of mercy.

Introduction

"As a man thinks, so he is!"—Proverbs 23:7

"Those who are easily shocked should be shocked more often." –Mae West

"High truth is hard to swallow but sweet and easy isn't the price of maturity." –RWB

"Men are not flattered by being shown that there has been a difference of purpose between the Almighty and them. To deny it, however, in this case, is to deny that there is a God governing the world." –Abraham Lincoln

I am assuming you are probably Protestant, have read the entire Bible at least twice, have the self-awareness that you have heard the same sermons repeated but without the promised results, and know that you know orthodoxy *seems* dead, while charismatic *seems* lively and that neither *seems* to actually, effectually work… at deep levels.

Welcome, then, friends of God, readers of the Bible, discerners of sermons, connoisseurs of human archetypes and ruggedized proto-saints and scoundrels aplenty! God wants us to grow from milk to meat! Sound interesting?

This book is for you, perhaps! If not, put it back on the shelf for a later, more blessed time. We all need to grow, and we all need to ask God to give us his mercy!

If you *still* believe this book might be for you, then great! There actually is a difference—a powerful difference—between humans in the milk of Christianity and humans in the meat of Christianity.

Those in the milk must have repeated the same, almost trite, stories of the Bible: David slaying Goliath, Jesus born in a crib, Paul "a-apostling" the Mediterranean, Joseph and his colorful coat, Moses in Egypt, etc. Each sermon, each lesson is given as if the audience hadn't heard it before, each is filled with good and nutritious milk. Everything is as it must be.

However, there actually is a relatively undiscovered country existing above the milk realm, and this meat territory in no way breaks scripture or God's many precepts. In fact, it does just the opposite. The meat territory of God fulfills the scriptures and God's many precepts even better than the milk does! Amazing, but true! True for every jot and tittle, as it were. Just like Jesus talked about.

Well, these are mighty big words, tall cotton, powerful talk. So then, does it work? Dear reader, the answer is: Yes, the meat territory works and works at vastly greater levels, powers, in communications with God, miracles, insight, wisdom, and even joy. Yes sirs, yes ma'ams, the meat territory works. Test it.

However, you need to be called to the meat territory. If nothing written on these pages makes sense to you, you are probably not yet called to understand the meat territory. Do us all a favor and don't fight this book, its pedagogy, its precepts, author, or adherents. Leave it be, if you can, until such time as you might later understand it.

Is this what is called having eyes to see spiritually, and ears to hear spiritually? Yes, I am afraid so. Sadly, I write this to you whom cannot *now* understand what is within the pages of this book. Happily, I write this to you whom *now maybe* can!

Time proves all things. Restated, time is a slow-motion truth detection machine. Let time prove whether or not the advanced material in this book is advanced or not. You will be doing yourself and God a favor, if you are able to let advanced concepts in Christianity prove to those with eyes

14

to see and ears to hear spiritually... if this book is a lie package, or true.

I can inform you, however, I have been at this task from 1994 to 2018 as I now write this, a time of 24 years. I am almost 65, and in truth have been at this task all my life. But the meat part of understanding advanced Christianity, started when I was 40... and you may find this hard to believe, but advanced teachings work every single time, except for the exceptions.

Advanced teachings are powerful... and power can be dangerous. Mature folk are supposed to be able to handle mature, or powerful things. Be warned, therefore, this book is not about gaming life, it is about being granted powerful wisdom, and it really shouldn't be mocked. Great power and wisdom, in truth, should be honored. So if it is at all possible, give honor unto whom honor is due.

Once a manager of a Christian book store in Reno said to me of the top-selling Christian books, "These books offer quick, ineffectual solutions to the lost." Milk solutions don't really solve much, they exist for a reason, to protect the immature.

What is the source material for all this work? You might want to, at times, refer to the website www.inthatdayteachings.com. This is the source material. Mostly, they are poems. Why? Poetry is an advanced language *(i.e., higher)*. Poetry can reveal deeper meanings, and provide profound explanations... in a few short pages, compared to 50 or 100-page-long chapters. As a mercy to all, God provided poems.

How did the poems come about? As mentioned above, my awakening into the undiscovered territories (of meat vs.

milk Christianity) started in 1994. I was told perhaps a journal or diary would edify folks later. Well, the first decade was, for me, necessary confusion and conversion. Then around 2007, poetry came out in me. And that ended up being an excellent journal or diary, as God's Spirit gave me unction and zeal to pursue with vigor the multitudinous problems manifesting themselves in *this* form of Protestant Christianity, then *that* form, the *other* form and *many other* forms necessary for me to eventually explain, via this journey, to those who must need be later understanding meat Christianity.

I have mentioned "undiscovered territory." Actually, the more precise term would be the "restoration of all things." There is very little new under the sun, as Solomon noted. However, modern seminary and preachers have been so obtuse, so immature, so willingly blind to maturity… that rediscovering ancient truths or ancient paths (of Jeremiah 6:16) *seem* to be "undiscovered territory."

In truth, those in the enlightenment business are trail makers… who only rediscover ancient trails covered by debris, growth, neglect, enmity, and opprobrium avoidance.

What, then, am I doing with this body of work? My quest, as it turns out, was to see what's wrong, and do what's right. My job has been to make written material for all who seek to enter into the spiritual land above milk, which is meat, and to be a good guide. This work is a bridge from milk to the higher spiritual territory. Paul called it meat.

Know also that in every realm, there are thirds. There is the bottom third, middle third, and top third. This is true for the milk realm. For centuries, leaders at the top third of milk have poked their naughty heads into the bottom third of the meat territory and come home with microscopic nuggets of manna to brag about! Sure, this is what they do when stuck at that top milk realm. *Good on them?*

But dear reader, God gave me mercy to explore the bottom, middle, and top ranges of the meat territory. Granted, I am far from worthy. But it was necessary for this job of explaining things to you. So, I kind of have been there and done that. (What is above the meat realm? Answer: inscrutable things that cannot be described to us now in the milk or meat realms. Sufficient is the task for us to learn the milk and meat. *"Don't immanentize the eschaton!"* as Eric Voegelin said.)

Trust the plan, as Q says. Trust, if you are called to it, that you can learn High Teachings of Meat Christianity!

In short, have faith, read this book, trust and test what it says, and see what you can do. You might first be in denial, then anger, then try to bargain terms, then be depressed, then accepting. Saying goodbye to milk, and hello to meat involves such.

And... pray God have mercy on us all.

(Throughout this book, you will find references to my source material, www.inthatdayteachings.com. The title of a poem or think piece will be given. Simply go to the website, then the correct web page—or Book Number (There are 12 books, books #9 through #12 are on the home page). Next, use your web browser and search for the poem's title. For example, see www.inthatdayteachings.com, Book #3, Search "Dance with Me.")

Dear reader, as an example, this poem will be printed for you below, the rest of the time you will want to go to www.inthatdayteachings.com, find the Book Number and search in your browser for the poem title.

Dance with Me
(A Tale of the Christ)

By Robert Winkler Burke
Book #3 of "In That Day Teachings"
Copyright 11/12/02 www.inthatdayteachings.com

I can dance with the air,
I can dance without care,
But I can't dance with you,
When you're gone.

I can dance with the trees,
I can dance with the breeze,
But I can't dance with you,
When you're gone.

Oh when will you see,
My love is for thee?
But I can't dance with you,
When you're gone.

I'm there by your side,
Along every ride,
But I can't dance with you,
When you're gone.

When the world makes you think,
And fill up full with its drink,
Then I can't dance with you,
When you're gone.

But come back now to Me,
And be all you're to be,
And I'll dance with you,
As We have done.

Yes dance my love with Me,
The way life's meant to be,
And I'll dance with you,
As We have done.

The birds will rejoice,
Seeing you on your course,
When I dance with you,
*As We have done.**

---

*(See www.inthatdayteachings.com, Book #3 "Dance with Me")

Part I—Believe It: Possible/Line Upon Line/Learn the Comms

"When I Return, Will I Find Faith?"
—Luke 18:8 (Modified)

"Gird your sword on your side... in the cause of truth, humility, and justice."—Psalm 45

*B*elieve it is possible. Believe that there is, indeed, a meat *(i.e., mature)* territory above the milk purview now prevalent in most seminaries and church leaders. When it comes to **the meat understanding of Christ-in-You,** *"... the prophets take over and stumble all night... My people are ruined because they don't know what's right or true."*— *Hosea 4:6:10, The Message.*

But who has faith for true Christ-in-You? Those called to the territory above milk, that is who. And it will take all the faith you have, and even more! But it is doable.

The pedagogy is different in the meat territory compared to the milk. Milk endlessly repeats known sermons or stories. Usually, they involve three points. Sermon outlines provide these points. Even seminars will do the same. All milk.

In the meat territory, the teaching is different. It is line upon line, here a little, there a little, precept upon precept, this meme, that truth, another concept, etc. *(See Isaiah Chapter 28. Shockingly, there are perhaps thousands of points or lessons to learn, absorb, and become. It is not so much what you do, but who you are!)*

This is how the universe of the mind works. There are those *without* eyes and ears to hear spiritually, and those *with* them. The milk group is given parables. The meat group has the parables explained to them. It is not as easy to understand as you might think! Those in the meat often have to *give* parables, in order to be understood... in order to communicate higher thoughts or the meat disciplines.

And yes, it does take a lot of discipline to enter into the meat realm. One would do very well to engage simultaneously in ruggedization fitness programs. As the body, so the soul and spirit! *(See www.russianmartialart.com for Systema!)* Often, we will be like the poor father of the demon-filled child: *"I believe... help thou mine unbelief!"* Fortunately, the precepts, lines, memes, truisms, ways, and maxims of the meat realm can be tested. Learn them. Try them. Test them.

At first, it may seem that high teachings fail. Often, one precept is used wrongly by the newbie. It takes a while to figure out what works, why, and under what conditions. Nothing can usually be forced. Everything has to flow. You need to be using the right tool for the right conditions for the right problem and the right time. Seems like a lot? Yes, indeed, it is a lot.

What are three base, or bad emotions? Could they not be fear, greed, and laziness? What if I were to tell you that humans communicate by text and sub-text? Meaning to say the words spoken and the emotion or spirit under those words. I could sedately whisper, "Run out of here," to an audience in a theater on fire. I could also in a panic scream, "Run out of here!" In the two examples, the text is the same. But antipode *(underlying-subtext)* spirits are used.

So, it goes with preaching and living. God made our world such that we speak and hear two things simultaneously: the text and the spiritual subtext. Evangelical seminaries don't like to teach this, because their graduate preachers are famous for preaching the text of the Bible with a prosperity give-to-get greedy spirit; or preaching the text of the Bible with an end-times-dispensational fear spirit; or preaching the text of the Bible with an overwhelmingly insane, emergent-seeker-friendly spirit of unmitigated sloth and energy-robbing dissipation. *(Why? It sells. It itches ears of low-consciousness folk?)*

Jesus said to his disciples, "Ye know not what spirit ye are of." *(i.e., text and subtext.)*

In Advanced Christianity, you must always know the text in operation currently happening, along with whatever subtext spirit goes underneath. You might ask yourself continually, "Am I doing the right thing that God wants me to do in spirit and truth?"

In the current vernacular, this is known as being "a major dude." It is known as being the hero, or the smart player, the Jedi, the wise one who isn't conned like most people are.

Jesus taught that a more mature people know… "We worship God in Spirit and Truth." Ask yourself continually what spirits are in operation in the text (truths, semi-truths, and lies) and subtext (character and emotion) … in yourself and in all others. Also, with your two-way radio, you can be in continual connection and communication with God, who can explain what exactly is going on in spirit and truth, and what to do about it.

Like Christ 2,000 years ago, In That Day Teachings bravely, confidently, and thoroughly confront the mistakes of the religion of the day. Are any pastors curious? *(Have they avoided rebuke?)* These high teachings not only identify what Evangelical Christian leaders are doing wrong, and what they are missing by doing wrong, these teachings exquisitely proffer the corrective medicines… they enable the ameliorating right things to do… in order to not miss Christ-in-You by a mile, but rather enable spiritual abodes the possibility of good God indwelling!

(Granted… some current leaders <u>understand some elements</u> of meat territory and Christ-in-You. But a thorough search (autist-style, as Q followers can do) of the internet for Christian leaders, sermons, churches, seminaries, books, speeches, conferences, or any such related thing will prove to honest, capable, and disinterested minds… that prior to In That Day Teachings, no body of work explains the many ramifications, conclusions, unction, and amelioration into the restored arenas of high-level, (meat) Christ-in-You manifestation sufficient for God's epic day of denouement, great awakening and liberty!)*

---

*(See www.inthatdayteachings.com, Book #4, "Regarding the Fine Art of Caring")
(Book #6, "Blindly Inglorious, Proudly Incurious")
(Book #8, "Pastors, Take the Bitter Medicine")
(Book #10, Search "I Want to be Taught by Pastors… Altogether Incurious!")
(Book #11, Search "(Gulp!) Shall We Dance?")
(Book #12, Search "In That Day… Ends the End of the World! Oh Joy!")

"Believe in God's Prophets; So, Shall Ye Prosper." — 2 Chronicles 20:20 Modified

"Bad doctrine creates evil that evil inhabits and expands; while good doctrine creates good that God inhabits and expands." –RWB

"Right is right even if no one is doing it; wrong is wrong even if everyone is doing it." –Saint Augustine

"Victorious warriors win first and then go to war, while defeated warriors go to war first and then seek to win." – Sun Tzu

Bad prophets have *bad* answers; *good* prophets have *good* answers. Amplified: milk prophets submit under milk pastors and entertain their milk congregants; meat prophets never submit to milk leaders; rather, they correct the many errors of milk leaders.

Sadly, milk church and seminary currently provide virtually no meat prophets. Therefore, they cannot with authority tell you whether rapture's fear preaching, or prosperity's greed preaching, or emergent's lazy preaching is okay. Because there currently are only milk seminaries, only milk pastors (with a few exceptions), and only milk prophetic schools, churches, and seminar circuits... none in this category can tell you whether selling fear, greed, or laziness under the Bible's text is good or hokum.

Thankfully for you, dear reader, I can tell you prophetically that rapture is wrong, prosperity give-to-get is wrong and emergent's lazy dogma is wrong. They are all wrong. Wrong. Wrong. Wrong. There now, I have said it. *(Wrong stops Christ-in-You!)*

You can test this, by the way. However, it has already been tested by multitudes stuck in milk. Good fruit does not come from a bad tree. This is sad news, indeed! But thankfully, good fruit does come from a good tree.

If you have eyes to see, dispensational sermons have no anointing, no healing, no ability to provide the listener with higher precepts... just mainly fear is provided. Maybe something from a headline from the Jerusalem News Post? *Yawn.* Who cares? Maybe the end of the sermon will fearfully ask who in the audience is not ready to be whisked away from misery on Earth? These fear-based altar calls are kind of weird, are they not? Weird and predictable.

You know the best generals are unpredictable. And their soldiers love their generals for being unpredictable. It is how leadership truly leads and provides winning battles for the troops. Did you know God is a Man of War? Well, he says he is in Exodus 15:3. And what is the Lord of Hosts? That would be the leader of leaders, the general of generals, wouldn't it be Jesus? Wouldn't it be God?

The best general has the battle won before it starts, and even has the war won before the battles start. The bulk of the winning is done before engaging with the enemy. So it is with God. So it is with this book. Learn here, do later.

The carnal reaction of milk believers who are called to learn meat teachings is a) Denial, b) Anger, c) Attempts to negotiate, d) Depression, and e) Acceptance. It is so depressing for milk managers of religion to realize they have missed it by a mile.

God have mercy on us all!*

---

*(See www.inthatdayteachings.com, Book #3, Search "Captain of the Be")

(Book #3, Search "I am a Man of the Cloth")

(Book #12, Search "Why Don't They Ask a True-Doctrine Prophet About Doctrine?"

"Every Man I Meet Is My Superior in Some Way..."
—Ralph Waldo Emerson

"Leaders who say you have everything to learn from us, but we have nothing to learn from you... are erroneous." –RWB

"In Milk Christianity, there is no opprobrium correcting it, only ersatz-OPs?" –RWB

*W*hat does higher pedagogy mean? It means humility, it means patience to learn hundreds or thousands of points of light. It means waiting until some point there is a sufficiency of lessons learned that the "boat gets up to plane," as it were.

It means the teacher will get frustrated with the students, the students will get frustrated with the teacher, and everybody will be frustrated with God himself! Only: believe, believe, and carry on… students will see the power of God in the teacher, the very presence of God in the teacher, the powers of healing and otherwise in the teacher… so the students have to believe, well… we can learn to be like that also if God has mercy!

Note that the milk road of religion is an okay road, but it only goes so far. This is by design, for it protects the small from the big, to use an expression. However, the meat road of Christianity goes everywhere you'll ever need to go spiritually.

Meat Christianity is not necessarily in enmity to milk religion, it is entirely congruous… except to milk Christianity's many sins of wayward behavior.

The first sin of milk religion is not permitting the existence of meat. It over-evangelizes, to extreme moronic outcomes. Milk religion seems to be a motor without a governor. It races wildly, hither and yon, unchecked by anything. In milk religion, there are few—if any—checks and balances. Milk leaders suppose themselves rather perfect, despite the implosions of milk leaders granted popularity and power.

In short, milk religion is pride, religious pride. The step into meat Christianity involves a guillotine of pride. Lose the religious pride, gain Christ-in-You. That's how it works. Restated: *Save Face, Lose Christ-in-You Life!*

Milk religion tends to be not only overly proud but also overbearing, over-lording, too simplistic, rigid, fixed-rule-based regarding money extraction from congregants, repeating simple things over and over, formulaic, platitude-based, acrostic-insane, bromide-filled, infantile-simplistic, babyish-in-delivery, promoting three bad emotions of fear-greed-laziness, Mandarin in organization, absent God's power, absent God's healing, absent God's higher mind, absent God's higher sight and hearing, setting up congregants to be slaughtered by politicians, and absent God's greater realities.

Fortunately, there is a cure. God wants perhaps 5% of churches and seminaries… to break into the Ancient Paths of wisdom, the modern-day undiscovered territory of overflowing, percolating, always-surprising, abundantly ameliorating, God-synchronizing, unboundedly-epic, greater-works enabling, high levels of manifesting: Christ-in-You. *(See Jeremiah 6:16)* [*]

---

[*] (See www.inthatdayteachings.com, Book #4, Search "Breaking Off Adhesions"
(Book #6, Search "In That Day Unbound")

Sufficient for the Task, not Perfect: As Much as Is Enough!

"If you polish and wax a car too much, the paint goes away." –RWB

"Do not be too moral. You may cheat yourself out of much life so. Aim above morality. Be not simply good, be good for something." –Henry David Thoreau

*M*ilk teaching often seems somewhat digital, meaning on or off... no percentages. Meat teaching seems to be the reverse, mostly percentages and very little on and off.

In milk teaching, a person is either saved or not saved. Leaders in milk teaching tend to be evangelists, who believe all others in the body of Christ should also be evangelists bringing in the lost. There seems to be no "motor governor" on such leaders, they act like it is an "all-out war" to bring in the lost, and then have those who just came in, to go out and bring in the lost, rinse, and repeat ad infinitum.

Interestingly, in meat teaching, a person is usually concerned if the pastor or leader of the Christian group is saved, so crazy sometimes such leaders behave! Ha! But once past that, the worldview of a meat Christian tends to see things on an analog scale from zero to one or 0% to 100%.

How much did Jesus know of Father God? Answer: 100%. All other humans know Father God from 0% to something less than 100%. Even your pastor, even you or me.

An immature person, if asked to do a difficult task... will either say to the master, "Yes, I'll go," and then not go... or say, "No, I won't," but then later will. In these two biblical examples, the first response is the digital one (yes) and later the digital zero (no)… and then the other example is the digital opposite: zero (no) and later one (yes). Likewise, if trouble is encountered, if failure happens, if the journey gets difficult, the immature person threatens the master with, "I quit!" (Digitally: zero, or no.)

However, in meat Christianity, the more mature view things in percentages. See the advanced 2007 Western movie "3:10 to Yuma" wherein the mature character played by Russell Crowe likes certain things about a person, and dislikes certain other things about that same person. This is advanced thinking and being. "Here's what I like about you," and, "What I don't like about you." This is separating the bone from the marrow, muscle, and sinew. It also can involve picking out the dead things in a body which shouldn't have dead things in it! Matthew 24:28 says, "For wheresoever the carcass is, there will the eagles be gathered together" … to pick the ugly things out of the milk believer destined to be a proto-meat Christian. This is actually how it works. Not a lot of fun, but doable.[*]

_____

[*](See www.inthatdayteachings.com, Book #4, Search "Breaking Off Adhesions")
(Book #4, Search "An Advanced Degree in Thinking")

Imparting Does not Work Immediately, but Preachers Try

"I'll gladly pay you Tuesday for a hamburger today." – Wimpy from Popeye comic.

"No matter how many times Lucy pulls the ball away, will Charlie Brown learn?" –RWB

*"C*ome get your red-hot imparting!" say preachers, prophets, and conference speakers. If only it were true! But it isn't that easy!

Jesus taught his disciples for three years, then in John chapters 14–17, he said that after his departure, the Holy Spirit would come to teach all things. So, the disciples *still* had a lot to learn!

When Elisha got Elijah's coat of "double portion…" the two had traveled together for how long? Joshua and Caleb did pretty well for themselves and God, but only after how many years spent with Moses?

Believe, dear reader, in shortcuts all you want! And give *beaucoup* money to the short-cut prophetic leadership crowd. In fact, at their insistence, you can give double money, and get double the impartation and anointing? You will only waste your time and money if you want to learn the meat of Christianity.

Here is how it works. Suppose you meet a truly great, ascendant Christian teacher. He or she gives you a little cross of Jesus. It ain't going to make you a master! Fine, it is a fine gift. On the other hand… suppose you are joined at the hip with this great Christian teacher for a decade or so. When you are ready to also become a master teacher of the high country of God, your teacher gives you a little cross of

Jesus. Yes, that little cross of Jesus comes with a lot of power. But the strange thing is this. You could then lose that little cross, and you would realize it does not matter because the resident power of "Christ-in-You" is now in you.

True discipleship in the meat country, is a very, very rare thing. In milk Christianity, they have discipleship trainers to burn! This is why God wants 5% of churches in a city or seminaries in a nation… to teach meat, not milk.[*]

---

[*](See www.inthatdayteachings, Book #6, Search "What Shall Revival Be?")
(Book #6, Search "In That Day Unbound")

"Believe in the Goodness of Good."
Roy Masters

"It is difficult to get a man to understand something when his salary depends on his not understanding it."

—Upton Sinclair

*S*uppose a preacher loves to talk in a "preacher's voice" to the public. What does it mean? It means the man isn't comfortable, apparently, speaking in public in his normal voice? The man isn't comfortable in his own skin? Is the voice a shenanigan-clericalism ruse?

Further, this preacher who loves to speak using a "preacher's voice" in public... seems to think his knowledge of God, *by everyone accepting his "preacher's voice" ...* is above that of his audience? Far above? How far above everyone is this preacher?

But imagine now if, in that preacher's audience, Jesus Christ himself walked in with flowing white robe and sandals! After the preacher's talk is finished, suppose Jesus humbly said to this preacher, "Walk with me."

Jesus asks him, "What are you thinking, using that 'preacher's voice?'"

Can the preacher reply to Jesus using the "preacher's voice?" *No, no, he cannot.* Why? Because Jesus is above, or superior, in every way to this man. This man cannot from above preach down to Jesus, using the "preacher's voice." The man is humbled.

But what does this mean in everyday parlance? The preacher actually stinks at preaching. Ipso facto, or by the very fact and act as an inevitable result: he does not believe

40

any person in the audience in the past, present, or future is equal or above himself!

But what does this really mean? It means this preacher probably loathes, hates, detests, and will reject: Christ-in-You! *(The very thing he is to enable in us?)*

Hence, a preacher preaching in an overlord "preacher's voice" isn't yet in Christ-in-You. Why? Christ-in-You is comfortable in your skin, and your voice has authority.

As Jesus said, "Be careful how you hear." This means to accept the text of the truth from anybody, but measure the underlying spirit and emotion... and if that underlying spirit or emotion is bad... then reject that bad spirit; but rather accept any good text! *(See Jesus tempted by the Devil in the desert.)*

It takes a lot to believe in worshipping God in spirit and truth. Our example of the "preacher's voice" indicates this man spoke God's text to the audience, but his overlord preacher's voice indicates his spirit is off. *(It lacks "now" synchronization with God.)*

People who cannot believe in the goodness of good, often live in a miserable world of good text and wrong spirit. The result can sometimes be extreme narcissism, wherein the narcissistic person believes God good, but everything and everybody else is bad, themselves excluded somehow! Many fundamental preachers fall into this archetype category. They believe God good, themselves the same, but you and all else in the word: sinners!

Truly, it is easy to miss Christ-in-You by a mile. The path is indeed narrow. Few there be that find it!

But this path is not Gnostic, meaning nobody "gets it" but some elite crowd who say you will never "get it," but they—via mysterious processes—do "get it." No, In That Day Teachings are not Gnostic, not a cult and not impossible to learn.

Why? Because Christ-in-You proves himself in others daring to believe in meat territory above milk. Why? Because this is how the saints did it, do it and will continue to do it. This process has always been there, available… but since Christ's ascension… it is even more available! Plus, we now live in a time when God seems to be desiring a vast increase in the numbers of meat Christians.

Hence, truths of "In That Day Teachings" are a sword like no other! Hence, this introductory book, "Think!—Like an Advanced Christian." Hence, this book references 12 In That Day Teachings books on the author's website. Hence the line upon line pedagogy and poetry are higher language devices able to communicate more than prose.

Bottom line, God has gone to a lot of trouble to make Christ-in-You available worldwide via "In That Day Teachings" at minimum expense and maximum effect! Seminary provosts, Christian leaders, or frustrated *Out-of-Churchers* are you interested?

Ask yourself these questions: Do in That Day Teachings explain much? Do in That Day Teachings prove themselves true over time? Do in That Day Teachings explain how milk seminary, church, and Bible studies are stuck in endless loops of milk shenanigans? If time keeps proving In That Day Teachings true, shouldn't seminary, church, and Bible study leaders be curious? Why aren't they curious? Have God's people prayed for a solution for hundreds of years? Has God arranged answers to those prayers? Should anybody, then, honor In That Day Teachings? What would happen if seminary, church, and Bible study leaders honored and practiced the truths in In That Day Teachings?*

---

*(See www.inthatdayteachings, Book #6, Search "What Shall Revival Be?")

(Book #11, Search "Who Prays for Solution and Rejects Solution?" (Book #11, Search "(Gulp!) Shall We Dance?")

(Book #12, Search "We Are the Best Preachers in This World, The Next… and Any!")

Who Said That Seminaries Should Require Reading Poetry? Answer: Eugene Peterson, The Message Bible

To understand the gullible nature of congregants and pastors, study the book and films of "Elmer Gantry" by Sinclair Lewis. Study the 1997 film "The Apostle" with Robert Duvall. Study as a contrast the Russian language (English subtitle) 2006 film "The Island."

"We compete with everything that occupies the mind of a child." –toy manufacturer

*T*his book is a swing-for-the-fence, Hail Mary-pass, and eleventh hour-minute effort for the Body of Christ subsumed by milk doctrines from seminary, pulpit, conference, and Bible study operations.

Previously, 12 In That Day Teachings (ITDTs) books were made to explain perhaps 1,000 memes or points of light necessary to travel from milk darkness to light purity and potential Christ-in-You indwelling.

This then is the 13th book from In That Day Teachings: *Think!—Like an Advanced Christian.* It is amazingly short, not too recondite, not too heavy to lift mentally or spiritually... but hopefully like Goldilocks' porridge in the bear cabin... just right!

This book gives meal-sized portions in small-bite sections. Each section starts, as you see, with a snappy quote, headline or riddle. Sections are a page or three long.

Each section then is foot-noted with references to the author's magnum opus www.inthatdayteachings.com website of 12 ITDTs books, which mostly contain poetry. This work is epic in scale, like Virgil's... but whereas he strove to explain Rome's divine destiny, ITDTs demystify how—*before Christ otherwise returns*—<u>why, when, wherefore, how, and in whom he returns as Christ-in-You!</u>

The references ask the reader to go to the correct book page on the website and then use the browser search function to find the referenced work. *(i.e., Press Control or Command and "F" keys simultaneously.)*

In this fashion, this book is more like 13 books, making the large pedagogy of meat Christianity available and doable. All in all, the production of this book and its 12 website-referenced books, along with additional references to high-thought texts from others *(i.e., Lincoln, Founding Fathers)* is quite a feat! This awesome mind geography is befitting the Mind of Christ since intelligence is as intelligence does and intelligence liberates slavery!

What in the past could only be done by personal High Discipleship, can now possibly be done by diligent Christians worldwide. All in all, the process is similar to the Q or Qanon phenomena of thousands of points of light (posts on www.qanon.pub)… designed to ask questions, engage readers with "open source" searches on the internet to confirm the (Berean) truths therein… in order to gain confidence in the enlightenment process (trust The Plan) and quicken souls to big events (The Calm Before the Storm… and The Storm) in order to go "From Darkness to Light" and cause a cleansing (Drain the Swamp) via an ameliorating (Enjoy the Show) upgrade program (called

The Great Awakening). Q tells us repeatedly to "use logic" and "expand your thinking." Indeed.

Sound too heavy to lift? Sound too recondite? Sound impossible? Trust the Plan. Why was this book written? Answer: To enable Christ-in-You.

Don't milk seminaries, milk churches, and milk books *already* enable Christ-in-You? No, sadly the milk operations mostly obviate, prevaricate and do the antipode of Christ-in-You promulgation. *They cannot help but do so!* (Milk leaders play whack-a-mole to real meat Christians when discovered? Such leaders act always as one-way diodes, never do they want reciprocity or the idea of them stooping down to learn from a Christ-in-You indwelt one?) What if God wants about 5% of seminaries and city churches to offer meat paths to Christ-in-You? Why? So that in the future perhaps 5% of Christians would be *in the meat of Christ-in-You!* This is not a wicked operation, just the opposite.

What would happen then? Well, bad doctrines would be understood to be ineffectual by the proofs of working two-way radios in Christ-in-You folk who chuck bad ideas. Next, Christ-in-You Christians would be significantly synchronized with God and all good, while just as significantly in measured enmity against all that is bad... since Christ-in-You is something of a mind-meld with God, the universe's greatest thinker!

Ideally, reputable, established seminaries... ought to be publishing all 13 ITDTs books *(even with illustrations!)* and offer them broadly as part of the seminary curriculum worldwide. These books would also be handsome for existent church leaders themselves, as well as for individuals wishing to drink deeply the mature nature of Christ-in-You.

Enjoy!*

---

*(See www.inthatdayteachings, Book #3, Search "Light 'Em Up!")

(See www.qanon.pub, Search and read from first date (bottom) to most recent (up.)

(See www.inthatdayteachings, Book #1 and read through it.)

Part II—Two Way Radio/Ring of Truth/Test Everything

"You Know Truth When You Hear It." — *Greg Hunter*

*T*ruth has a certain ring to it. Have people forgotten this? Back in Christ's day, they had not. "… the people were astonished at his [Jesus'] doctrine: For he taught them [i.e., spoke to them] as one having authority, and not as the scribes."—Matthew 7:28-29 KJV

If you say out loud, "I am actually a Martian, born on Mars, and I have green skin and I am eight feet tall and three inches" … well, it should sound to your ears like a lie. If you, on the other hand, say out loud your true name, birthplace, and height… well, it should sound to your ears like the truth.

The truth has a resonance, a resoundingly deep and authoritative sound. Lies sound cracked. Like fingernails on a chalkboard. Like a "screechy, cracked" voice. Learn the difference.

What are we doing here? We are endeavoring to get our two-way radios working in good order. What two-way radios? The ones that are in each person, invisible, but connected with our Creator, God himself, who made it a two-way communication device. Use it. It is life unto you. It is wisdom.

The Old Testament puts it this way, "Hearken unto the voice of the Lord." The New Testament puts it this way, "Blessed are those who hear my words and obey."

What damages our two-way radios? Answer: the wrong doctrine believed. What repairs our two-way radios? Getting out bad doctrine, and putting in good doctrine.

Stated differently, bad Christian doctrine is similar to taking a five-pound hammer and busting up a nice tabletop two-way radio. On the other hand, good doctrine can be like putting in all-new parts in a broken radio and making it perform better than ever.

This is why doctrine counts. Correct doctrine is life unto you. Bad doctrine: death.

And you can test whether doctrine is good or not. Go ahead and believe every rapture minister, author and conference headliner in their faith in rapture. Your radio will not work hardly at all! Go ahead, try this!

Then, try believing what is in this book. Over time, you will find your two-way radio is working better and better! Again, time proves all things. Time is like a slow-motion truth detection machine. Our same God has made a universe in which truth is proved true, and lies are proved false. You just need those eyes and ears to see and hear spiritually, that is all. (Again, the chicken and egg situation? Which came first? It doesn't matter in this case; you need both at the same time.)

Restated, you need both the knowledge of good and bad doctrine while also experimenting to prove doctrines by the ability you discern in your two-way radio with God. Good doctrine makes the radio work great! Bad, bad. Got it?

Step back and consider the ramifications of enabling your two-way radio with God. It means this is not a cult, as the top man is God! It means people in the meat of Christianity are synchronous. They abide with God and each other! And they/we ask to be checked!

It means we are more or less at one with the Universe and its Creator! We then can be in proper, measured harmony with all that is good, and discordant in measured behavior with all that is bad. In other words, God controls the dial.

You are known for the love you have for one another. You will often meet people whom you know are family... family of God. *(See John 13:35)* [*]

---

[*](See www.inthatdayteachings.com, Book #3, poem "What's wrong with this coin?"

The Ring of Truth

By Robert Winkler Burke
Book #3 of In That Day Teachings
Copyright 1/15/06 www.inthatdayteachings.com

Good

Friend, did you

Know for whom the bell

Tolls? It tolls for souls so well.

Each lie that is told and told bold

Each lie that is loved and then sold

Diminishes your spirit, if truth be told.

Truly, lies cannot but sound a bad knell

But the sound of truth, it rings a clear bell.

I pray

Can you tell?

If you can tell truth resonates like a heavenly bell,

And lies crack like a twisted, conniving, broken hell.

Then you will

Do well.[*]

---

[*]("Question him [the boy warning us of danger] no more,
Darrin," said King Lune. "I see truth in his face…" –The Horse
and His Boy, Chronicles of Narnia by C. S. Lewis.)

The Universe is built such that it continually proves truth to be true and lies to be untrue. Tells are everywhere, via eyes to see and ears to hear spiritually.

*I*nvisible Stage Dummy—Due to the nature of the universe and due to the nature of God… an errant preacher will occasionally display an "invisible stage dummy" that proclaims the embarrassing truth of his or her errant ventriloquist. Strange but true. It is the nature of Mark 16:20, which works forward and reverse, positive and negative. This should make all of us humans fear God. The universe, by no special effort, continually proves whether or not we are true or we are not, wise or idiotic, good or bad. It happens especially to teachers, who are held to a higher account. *(For eyes to see!) Restated, a seemingly invisible stage dummy will appear in (or with) a preacher on stage or while being interviewed who speaks truthfully, but in antipode, to the conventional lies, half-truths, or grey areas the preacher is used to making as a standard practice. It is the other voice of the speaker, the one that speaks truth in spite of that person's (top) conscience. The undercurrent, or the sub-text… will provide a true witness (eyes to see). Example? A (bad) POTUS will deliver a message outside in the Rose Garden, and a rat will walk (in broad daylight) in front of the podium. Example? A too tech'ed up ministry praise group (digital drums, electric (not acoustic) guitars, digital keyboards, digital violins) will have the electric* *power go out so that acapella brings anointing, not digital... as a witness. Will anybody have ears to hear what happened? Another example might be the plethora of hyper-grace preachers who preach and pray with hands in pants... usually, these preachers teach some kind of hyper-grace, and the universe responds, does it not?**

---

*(See www.inthatdayteachings.com, Book #8, Search "Kill My Invisible Stage Dummy!")

(Search the internet: "Why do men put hands in pants?")

Learn How to Go Out and Come In!

"In Dwelling, live close to the ground. In thinking, keep to the simple. In conflict, be fair and generous. In governing, don't try to control. In work, do what you enjoy. In family life, be completely present."—Lao Tzu

*W*hen you leave home, be well put together. Know what spirit you are of. Check your "heads up display" as to your physical condition: heart rate, core temperature, stiffness, flexibility, emotions, mental state, spiritual state … the whole spirit, soul and body, and the God connection and even, perhaps, unwanted connection to evil. Are you ready?

If you are not ready to leave your threshold, then do the work necessary to be ready. Also, this includes knowing what one is supposed to be doing when leaving one's threshold. What is the assignment? Is today a rest day? (Usually, one out of seven, not necessarily Sunday.) Who am I supposed to be prepared to meet? Am I ready for the assignment? Do I know what the assignment is? Is this going to be a mandatory surprise event? Okay, if you have to walk in unawares, so be it. Or do you already know the lay of the land? *(i.e., Is the stage set? And… "Action!")*

This sounds difficult, but it is doable.

People unaware of these concepts sometimes travel, or go to restaurants… in their pajamas! Likewise, that bent old person, that person unable to disconnect from the phone, the other one lost in a tablet game, the walking wounded, the living undead… these are all victims of milk life not lived well. In meat Christianity, you don't do this. You are aware, you are alive, you are present and, *"Reporting for Duty, Sir!"*

At the meat level, generally, you go out with one major objective. It is sufficient for the task to engage and do this major objective. Be warned that it is usually unwise to then also do other major or minor things. Simply go out, do the objective, come back in. To do more or less… involves rue or unwanted recompense. You are dealing, at times, with great power of the universe, a thing difficult to understand in verity. Only with the greatest maturity, should one dare to do multiple things when on assignment. It would be an exception to the rule. God have mercy![*]

---

[*](See www.inthatdayteachings.com, Book #11, Search "Shall We Dance?") Deut. 28:6

Large Computer Screens Needed!

"Where We Go One, We Go All!" —Qanon

*I*n That Day Teachings (ITDTs) are, indeed, a mind-expanding magnum opus. Like Paul's epistles, the scope is broad, the subjects are wide and deep, the considerations are many, the epic reach is biblical... and because of all these things, get yourself some large computer screens!

Due to the nature of the universe, large and mature thoughts are not easily communicated, understood, manipulated, or apprehended from the relatively tiny screens of smartphones, tablets, and laptops. To make the geography of your mind epic, study ITDTs with big screens! *(i.e., Large, complex movie ideas are understood better in big-screen theaters.)*

Just look at an Avenger movie when Tony Stark, Captain America, Dr. Bruce Banner, or Nick Fury want to think strategically, up pop very large holograph computer screens displaying large concepts. *Well, be like them.* Get a modern computer with one, two, or three large screens. Then, In That Day Teachings can more easily be understood and absorbed. Otherwise, improvise *(use what is available),* adapt *(adjust to new conditions),* overcome *(succeed!)* as the US Marines say.

As has been noted elsewhere, this book recommends that as you read it, to search the internet for various texts, YouTube videos, and—especially—ITDTs poems! Expand your thinking, this is what the meat territory of Christ-in-You is all about.

Also, surround yourself with God-approved, God-sourced goods. While God's approval certainly can change over time, consider classic Revere Ware, classic Chicago Cutlery, Ford vehicles, North Face equipment, Cross Century pens, classic World Bibles, Corning dishware, Colt firearms, Springfield Armory firearms, Kabar knives, Propper BDUs, Mercedes Benz, BOSE systems, Boeing aircraft, Wrangler wear, Michelin tires, Craftsman tools, DEWALT tools, Trek bicycles, Vibram soles, Apple devices, etc.[*]

---

[*](See www.inthatdayteachings.com, Book #11, Search "Shall We Dance?") Deut. 28:6
(See www.qanon.pub, Expand your thinking. Trust the Plan. WWG1WGA!)

Test: Un-Programming Yourself and Expand Your Thinking

"Here We Go!"—Donald Trump

"There are no fixed rules that God (and man) cannot break while keeping just." –RWB

*H*ow do you get In That Day Teachings started? Well, it helps to un-program yourself of whatever milk method, lines, ways, precepts, here a little, there a little… you are currently doing in the milk!

Restated, you cannot do the same thing and expect a different result! It may sound shocking, but when a qualified newbie (in Star Wars mythology: a Padawan, apprentice, learner) starts… the master will recommend stopping doing whatever it is that has that person stuck (in The Silver Chair, as C.S. Lewis might say—a magic spell, binding the person to low-level life).

How shocking would this advice be? Well, it might be to stop reading the Bible every day! Remember, there are no fixed rules, only guidelines. It might be to restrict Bible reading to the KJV, the Amplified and Eugene Peterson's The Message.

It might be to read out loud the red letters of Christ in the four Gospels, perhaps one hundred times. It might be to listen to The Message's New Testament at night maybe a thousand times.

It might be to move to another territory. It might be to live close to a running stream or river. It might be to start www.russianmartialart.com locally. It might be to study the double binding self-restraint liberty the Founding Fathers mandated. It might be to stop listening to bad-spirit music. And that might include stopping listening to wispy-voiced, ineffectual milk-praise Hypno-music. It might be to stop watching charismatic-NLP televangelists. It might be to stop attending audience-control via shenanigan Christian (so-called) conferences and prophetic (so-called) assemblies.

It might be to leave the milk church alone for a while. It might be to get a dog or sell your horses. It might be to get outside on some long wilderness trips. It might be to gain elevation literally by hiking into high altitude mountains.

It might be carrying a sub-compact Bible on your person. Strangely, if you can remain calm and kind, it might be carrying a knife, a gun, and a Bible (but only if you can remain absolutely kind at all times). *(Don't break any laws!)*

It might be becoming a patriot, and loving your country for the good it can possibly do.

It might be becoming comfortable in the skin of your body, the skin of your soul *(mind and emotions)* and the skin of your spirit *(learning to be congruent with God and good... while disconnected and properly discordant with all that is bad).*

It might take changing jobs.

It might take letting God scourge you, as per Isaiah 28. It is called "The Overwhelming Scourge." Fear God, dear reader, it is something to go through!

When these things happen, check with your two-way radio with God to be sure you are on the right track. God knows how to prove himself in these matters.

The High Teachings path involves not *man over-lording man*, not man scourging man, not man harming man… it involves a teacher showing how God might possibly take us through some tough things we need to host Christ-in-You in the meat realm.

Again, the process involves God doing his work with humans, not humans putting humans through some kind of carnal boot camp for saints. God does it better.[*]

---

[*](See www.inthatdayteachings.com, Book #3, Search "The Cracked Pot" and "King Self")
(Book #3, Search "I am a Man of the Cloth."
(See www.qanon.pub.)
(See Abraham Lincoln's 1838 "Lyceum Address," a synopsis of a great man's philosophy.)

Part III—Bad: Out/Good: In/Self: Control/God: Indwells

Until the Lord returns, This Is How the Lord Returns: Christ-In-You.

(Understand the aggregate of In That Day Teachings, and you will know Christ-in-You and whom says three times on the last page of the Bible, "Behold, I come quickly."— RWB)

*H*ow and when does the Lord return? Mysterious answer: Blessed are the pure in heart for they shall see God. Decoded answer: Until the Lord returns, this is how the Lord returns: Christ-in-You. And so, bless the man, woman, or child in whom you see Christ is happy to manifest. *(Hint: Biblically, it is like seeing faces in the clouds.)*

Of course, it takes eyes to see and ears to hear spiritually in order to really see in whom Christ is manifesting at significant levels. So, it is again asking which comes first, the chicken or the egg?

Would you like to manifest Christ-in-You in a big way? How do you get it started? First, bless someone else who is manifesting Christ in a significant (or even minor) way. Then it (Christ-in-You) perchance… redounds back to you. Restated, the process requires humility, and to bless another who is manifesting Christ-in-You… then that requires humility first. (Pastors seldom, if ever, salute and bless or encourage Christ-in-You manifesting in their congregants, for the reason of pride and ignorance of the process.)

Unless you say blessed is he or she who comes in the name [and surprising nature] of the Lord, [and how Christ surprisingly manifests] your spiritual house will remain desolate of God's indwelling, or Christ-in-You [due to lack of humility in regards to religious knowledge.] *(See the end of the 23rd chapter of Matthew.)*

It turns out God searches high and low for an abode to indwell. Even though God made this, that, and the other thing… what he is really looking for, is that humble, spiritual home to indwell. This home must be non-preachy, against clericalism, un-gullible, right-smart, flexible of mind, non-didactic, non-knee-jerking, non-reactionary, non-judgmental, accepting, non-bothersome, adapt, unflappable, self-controlled, graceful under pressure, having inner authority, surprisingly capable and holy-flexible as opposed to being rigid-righteous-annoying. *(See Isaiah 66:1-2. See Col. 1:26-27.)*

In regards to the many mentions of the return of Jesus in the Bible, if you are in the milk, you will take them literally. If you are in the meat, you can see that a good portion of the returns of Christ is to be taken as Christ-in-You.

Milk seminary, church, and Bible study leaders will fight to the death the notion that Christ-in-You can and does return now in good people *(That is, people they will refuse to honor… in fact they will persecute any such people! Such people they banish!)* Because these souls are in the milk, they cannot see it any other way. So, they breathlessly will repeat a known Bible story as if nobody ever heard it before, and they will not want to wait before they hear it again as if it were new to them. And such people are spiritually blind!

However, for people with spiritual eyes to see and ears to hear, Christ-in-You *does return* and that is how good is achieved, really tough problems are solved and life in this temporal realm advances toward heaven's plan.[*]

(See John 14:3. See also John 14:20 in the NASB and especially The Message.)

---

[*](See www.inthatdayteachings.com, Book #3, Search "And So I Return Quickly")

(Book #4, Search "How to Turn a Page (into Knight!)")

(Book #8, Search "Behold: Christ Comes Quickly in the Self-Aware!")

(Book #8, Search "Fighting Leviathan")

"Commandment One tells us to have no other gods, or ideas, or rigid-rules, or overlord mandates to make others tithe to us, or to otherwise box trap innocent humans into a cul-de-sac kill zone?"

–RWB

"Let right be done." – Old English common law saying

"To be wise, walk with the wise." – Proverbs 13:20

"A grape matures in the presence of another mature grape."– 1985 miniseries Lonesome Dove, from Larry McMurtry novel

*T*here Are No Fixed Rules—Don't make rules your God. Putting rules, even God's rules, above God is to break the First Commandment: *Thou shalt have no other gods before Me.* It takes maturity to grasp, but understand God is above the rules we set about Him. If He wants to write a new testament, do miracles today, stop doing miracles, manifest His Son in people, not do such and such, do such and such…well, let Him. He is God. We either make our rules subject to God's obedience or we are obedient to God our ruler. Sound unfamiliar? It shouldn't. The enemy of good must fear good's unpredictable good. The enemy of good wants good to believe good has only fixed rules, rules that the enemy of good, therefore, can easily exploit. But God, or good, is not that stupid. Only some of the wayward churches are that stupid, by their enforcing supposedly fixed rules of tithing that appear to be helpful to weak, self-interested, disconnected-from-God leaders. Exodus 15:3 says, *"The Lord is a man of war…"* The U.S. Marine Corps Tactics manual puts it this way: *"There are no fixed rules that can be applied automatically, and every situation is different… Leaders must remember that there are no fixed rules and no precise checklists, but there are bounds."* Gene

Autry put it another way in his song *Back in the Saddle Again*: *"And the only law is right."**

---

*(See www.inthatdayteachings.com, Book #4, Search "Stuck in Rigid Righteousness")

(Book #8, Search "And Another: Apologetic Apoplexy!")

Don't Ask Milk Church to Approve (or Fight) High Teachings.

"In history, did wheel inventors ask approval from shoemakers?"—RWB

*T*he first thing a newbie to meat Christianity will do is rush back to *milk* family, friends, and church leaders and then ask for the approval of *meat* Christianity teachings. The second thing a newbie to meat Christianity will do is enlist *milk* family, friends, and church leaders to fight against *meat* Christianity. *(Please, don't!)*

However, usually the urge is irresistible to the newbie in meat Christianity. Of course, the *milk* family, friends, and church leaders will not approve of the newbie learning *meat* Christianity. And the *milk* family, friends, and church leaders will fight against the *meat* Christians helping the newbie. *(God, forbid!)*

This is a very, very old game. Who crucified Christ? The religious leaders of the day got the Roman state to kill Jesus. Have mercy on your teachers, and simply learn the High Teachings, and don't ask milk family, friends, or church leaders to approve, as they will only want to fight your teacher.

Try to learn high teachings without making too much of a fuss. Suspicious milk Christians might enlist the State to prosecute you. *For so persecuted they the (holy men, women and) prophets which were before you. (Matthew 5:12b KJV)*

Best advice for Padawans? Have faith in the plan, believe high teachers, avoid cults and stay under the radar.[*]

---

[*](See www.inthatdayteachings, Book #3, Search "Who Killed the Christ?")

(Book #3, Search "Who Am I to Tell Them?")

(Book #4, Search "Advanced Degree in Thinking")

The Purpose of Life is to Hear from God,
"Well Done Thou Good and Faithful Servant."

"As a British officer in WWII, you could be a POW and build a bridge over the River Kwai for the Japanese... or you could blow it up if you weren't supposed to?"—RWB

*I*n the meat realm of Christianity, the purpose of life is to hear, "Well done thou good and faithful servant" from the Lord. This implies you have heard what the Lord wants you to do, you have asked him questions about it (with your two-way radio), and you did what God wanted, getting sufficiently good grades on the project!

Therefore, you must know how to make a decision. What is the best way? Turn aside and ask God. Then do what God wants. The thing must line up with not only you but Christ-in-You inside you, Father God who is inside Christ (inside you!) but also the Holy Spirit, who is on the Earth and teaches all things, and also scripture. All this comes together, and the actions will be wise. *(John 14:20)*

The teaching is to "Have no Opinion." The prophet Bob Jones taught this. You see, God has an opinion on everything. We would be wise to agree with that opinion. It helps us avoid doing things nugatory or antipode of God's will.

Restated, check in with heaven before doing something. This is also called praying continually, properly understood. Should you give a beggar money? What is God telling you to do? Yes? How much money should you give the beggar? Again, God can tell you, can he not? First, learn and do this with small things, like, "Should I buy this orange or that apple?" Let God's Spirit guide your mind, hand, and wallet. It is good to be under the *control* of the Holy Spirit *(vs. typical spirit-filled people: not under the Spirit's control).*

Small decisions are easier to allow God to operate in. Big decisions, like which home to buy, what job to get, whom to marry… these are tougher for a person to get God involved in. Again, have no opinion… first see what God's mind is on the matter! This also works with politics, by the way.

Emergency decisions can, therefore, be easy. In an emergency, turn aside and ask God what to do. Then do it. *This might take a lot of practice!*[*]

---

[*](See www.inthatdayteachings.com, Book #3, Search "To Decide Not to Decide")
(Book #3, Search "Give God a Chance")

How to Understand The (Cheap or Dear) Double Bind?

DOUBLE BIND: "A psychological predicament in which a person receives from a single source, conflicting messages that allow no appropriate response to be made [because the milk con usually presents a world without morals or higher essence]."

—Merriam-Webster's Dictionary

"Power corrupts, absolute power corrupts absolutely."
—Lord Acton

"Circus is a great show, but a little side act from God can be the greatest know."—RWB)

*D*ouble binds are fascinating. As a meat Christian, you must be familiar with the territory. Milk Christianity can involve leaders too-clever-by-half foisting double-binds upon their unbeknownst congregations, in order that all stay blind of eye spiritually, and all stay deaf spiritually. But this is not the case in mature Christianity. Here below, is a list of double bind situations either to avoid or appreciate their need.

Catch-*22*—A problematic situation for which the only solution is denied by a circumstance inherent in the problem, describing a tricky problem or a no-win or absurd situation. Joseph Heller explained that a WWII pilot didn't want to fly a bomber over Germany. It was crazy (supposedly) to fly, but no crazy pilots could fly, but if you said it was crazy to fly, then you were considered sane and made to fly. <u>This whole concept ignores duty, honor, and living for the greatest good.</u> In short, if you want to go stark, raving, hopelessly insane, believe in nothing and it will kill you. *(Why? Jesus said an "empty house" can't stay empty, demons will rush in to steal, kill, and destroy.)*

Whom to Kill on the Lifeboat—A teacher up to no good will present this problem to students too young to know the solution. The teacher presents a problem wherein survivors from a sunken cruise ship are on a lifeboat with so many passengers, with just half as much food as it takes to row to shore, without any other possibility of rescue or fish catching. Whom on the boat would you kill? The answer is to send this teacher to find some other moral occupation because such as these do not bolster Western Enlightenment's Liberty memes, laws, precepts, ideals, and truths. In history, it is well known that some very brave men and staff of the Titanic gave their lives, and went down with the ship so that women and children had seats on limited lifeboats. In emergency situations, we are not God and we don't kill innocents. In emergency situations, meat Christians turn aside and inquire of God with their two-way radios and find out answers to the question, "What should I do?"

Fixed Rules—Milk leaders love fixed rules for their followers, but every leader should know they are exempt from fixed rules. A leader will stand and say, "Now everyone, please stand down and sit." But the ruler, standing, is exempt. The best militaries know that fixed rules will get themselves killed by the enemy. The US Marines teach that there are no fixed rules, only guidelines.

Turn to Your Neighbor and Say—Milk preachers who are charismatically inclined sometimes shout at their audience, "Turn to your neighbor and say, 'God is good!'" But think about this Double Bind! Isn't this a cacophony?

Why should all talk at once? Who listens when all speak? "Turn to your neighbor and say, 'It is rude to both talk at once!'" Better would be the preacher explain this ruse designed to install blinders, this ruse designed to remove eyes to see and ears to hear spiritually… *what a shenanigan is!*

Morals are, heh heh, Relative—This is the Progressive Ten Commandments all rolled into one expression. It is taught in public schools for the sake of tyrants, by tyrants, and for tyrants. Tyrants want their boots on the faces of people forever, and this is how.

No Proposition can be Proved True (Suckers!)—This is (also) the Progressive Ten Commandments all rolled into one expression. It is taught in public schools for the sake of tyrants, by tyrants, and for tyrants. Tyrants want their boots on the faces of people forever, and this is (also) how.

The Red Pill Problem—A people deceived by Church and State shenanigans and brainwashing rinse and repeat cycles… will demand three things of a truth speaker. First, the truth speaker must be silenced or banished. Second, the truth speaker must undergo psychological "dumb-thyself-down" programming. Third, drug the truth speaker. In Christ's time, they simply stoned or crucified truth speakers. Usually, the majority of religions got the State to do the dirty work? Nothing much has changed, has it?

Don't Cast Your Pearls Before Swine—This is a "dear" or "very good" double bind. When milk folk don't have eyes to see or ears to hear, don't cast your pearls of wisdom before them or they will turn and rend you. Did you know pigs eat humans? Sad, but true.

Does This Dress Make Me Look Fat?—This also is neither a good or bad double bind. Yet, and even so, don't ask it. Don't answer it. Any questions?

God Can Double Bind You—God once played the "Holy Fool" to double bind Moses. When the humblest person alive, perhaps had murderous thoughts toward his own rebellious, obtuse tribe... God picked up on those thoughts. He then offered Moses to forget all the promises he had made regarding the Hebrew's future... and told Moses he could kill them all, a million or two give or take, and crown Moses the heir apparent. Moses, shocked by this double-bind offer, realized to accept it would make God a liar (regarding promises made to the Hebrew tribe) and it would also hide the evil in his, of all people's, apparently wicked heart! If he, the most-humble, could be tempted by power's absolute corruption, then anybody at any time could likewise be corrupted! What a reveal! The Founding Fathers knew about this concept deeply. Moses declined the offer. The Founding Fathers, in their time... got busy, and made a nation of Liberty.

Federalist Paper #51—"But what is government itself, but the greatest of all reflections on human nature? If men were angels, no government would be necessary. If angels were to govern men, neither external nor internal controls on government would be necessary. In framing a government which is to be administered by men over men, the great difficulty lies in this: <u>you must first enable the government to control the governed, and in the next place oblige it to control itself</u>."—James Madison

In Liberty, We Must Double Bind Ourselves—James Madison said, "No man can be the judge in his own case." Tyrants teach "morals are, heh, heh, relative" so their boots smash faces, forever. Tyrants teach "the ends justify the means." They play god. We must not play god. Just because tyrants pretend to not believe in God, doesn't mean God doesn't want us to humanely, quickly, efficiently defeat tyrants who would kill all.

(Search 3 Documents: The Declaration of Independence, The US Constitution, the Bill of Rights. Study these vast, ameliorating things of Liberty's double-binding self-control.)

(Liberty is mutually pledging allegiance to Freedom's self-control and stopping them without within. This involves people being generally intelligent, moral, and lovers of laws and the US Constitution, Bill of Rights, and the 1776 Declaration of Independence.)

If It Was Easy, Everyone Would Do High Teachings.

"Usually, old wineskins can't receive new wine. Most old milk leaders cannot and will not see anything in the meat territory unless they are like Nicodemus in the night visiting Jesus. The problem is… old wineskins are now in virtually every teaching position? Yikes!"—RWB

("In truth, there are no flesh-manifested angels to organize anything. We must."—RWB)

*I*t is easier to apprehend the meat territory when sober. Drinking alcohol tends to reduce consciousness. Unless one is already quite bolstered, broadcast news can be deleterious. Harsh music can also make things difficult. Love-mush, weak and wispy praise can also be bad.

The first goal with In That Day Teachings (ITDTs) is to get bad out and get good in. The second goal is to keep bad out and keep good in—no small feat! The third goal is to do what is to be done in the High Country, so stay sharp. Only go where you are sent! Receive assignments, prepare, and do them! Flow, flow, flow with the percolation. Stay humble. Let God work through you.

Warning: Don't teach high teachings until released by God to do so. Almost all *Padawans* run out and teach too early. Don't.

The problem is that High Teachings increase power in you. Good is increased, but also bad. Therefore, you must get a higher percentage of bad out than folk in the milk ever bother with.

God sometimes can get bad out of a person by a thing called "the overwhelming scourge." It is a spiritual tumble in God's front-loading clothes washing machine and dryer. Survive it, don't resent it. (See Isaiah 28.)

God sometimes can get bad out of a person by having them lay down (spiritually speaking) and having Master Jedi eagles or vultures pick the dead things out of the surprised patient. Don't resent it, or them. Survive it, gain lessons learned. (Matthew 24:28)

God can also let massive failure do its cleansing work. Failure in marriage, family, finance, and business can happen. Anything can happen. Don't resent it. Survive it. Learn.

Also, Padawans want short contact with Masters; masters the reverse.

In the meat realm of operations, God can bond two souls on Earth, then one dies and goes to heaven... to seemingly send "measures of love" or vital resources to the remaining soul on Earth. This seems to be the case for David with Jonathan, for Paul with Stephen, for Elisha with Elijah, for Peter with James, for Jesus with John the Baptist. *(Us with Christ!)*

If all this sounds like hardball, well: God invented the game. Nothing is tougher, one supposes, than high country tough love. Remember, for those called to it... God considers *you rugged of character* (or needing to be so) and therefore, you are able to take what is being dished out for your own good. God doesn't want to give you hard treatment, but hard treatment (delivered by the harsh world) is sometimes the only thing that works.

Jump for joy, have cheer... so they also treated the prophets, saints, and holy folk who have gone before you. Don't worry, be happy.

Multitudes may be depending on you making it into the high realm. You can.[*]

---

[*](See 2014 Captain America film, where Steve Rogers is talking in barrack with professor.)

(See www.inthatdayteachings.com, Book #4, Search "Breaking Off Adhesions")

(Book #5, Search "When Lotsa Nobodies Believe Lotsa Nothing")

(Book #5, Search "All Souls Have Breaking Points")

(Book #5, Search "Life is a Double-Flowing Hourglass")

The Greatest Thing Ever Hidden in Plain Sight is Christ-In-You!

"How many light bulbs does it take to change a person?"

—*RWB*

"In That Day Teachings are well named, are they not?"

—*RWB*

*I*f you can believe In That Day Teachings (ITDTS) are real and that Christian reality does, in fact, occupy a milk territory and simultaneously a meat territory of Christ-in-You inhabitation… then you might enjoy the following *piece de résistance* explanation of scripture…

At the end of the Gospel of John, Jesus proceeds to rebuke Peter three times, asking that if Peter loves him, Jesus, then he must feed the sheep of Jesus. It is quite a rebuke. Peter and Jesus were walking together in this episode. Following close by, listening, was John the Apostle. Next, Jesus tells Peter how he is going to die as a martyr. Peter has had it! He turns around to see John and asks Jesus, "What about him? What is he going to do?"

Jesus says to John, "If I will that he tarry 'til I come, what is that to thee? Follow thou me." And John notes that this caused the disciples to broadcast the idea John wouldn't die, but John writes that Jesus didn't say John wouldn't die, but "If I will that he tarry 'til I come, what is that to thee?"

John ends the book by writing, "And there are also many other things which Jesus did, the which, if they should be written every one, I suppose that even the world itself could not contain the books that should be written. Amen."

With "meat" eyes to see, ears to hear spiritually, let us explain this masterpiece, magnum opus, masterwork, tour de force showpiece of how this territory actually works!

John the Apostle is an impressive person. He and his brother James—both fishermen—were called by Jesus the Sons of Thunder. The two had been earlier the disciples of John the Baptist. James died a martyr. John wrote the Fourth Gospel, The Three Epistles of John and the Book of Revelation. In all this, he grew in Christ-in-You.

In John 21, the resurrected Jesus is visiting his beloved disciples for the last time... in his resurrected flesh! High teachings indicate Jesus will later return as Christ-in-You! In this scene, we behold a) Jesus doing high-level meat work or correction, b) a recalcitrant Peter being obtuse, stubborn, shocked, unreceptive, and behaving at the milk, not meat level, and c) John the Apostle who—like Elihu—is already in meat territory position as scribe. Even so, John is a *snarky* scribe "rubbing it in" that all the while John was proudly "in the know" because after all, he is the disciple "whom Jesus loved... which also leaned on his breast at supper, and said, Lord, which is he that betrayeth thee?"

Right here, snarky young John is pouring salt on the wound! John is implying not only Judas betrayed Jesus the night before his crucifixion but also Peter who denied Christ three times*! (So, snarky John was in the meat, but the bottom-most third of it?)*

Peter, who in this scene is in the milk, was "cutting and dodging" and tried to direct Jesus to John, hoping perhaps Jesus would criticize John? Instead, Jesus says, 'If I will that he tarry 'til I come, what is that to thee? Follow thou me.'

Okay, Jesus is saying to Peter that in the future he will come in and live with Peter as Christ-in-You... and to worry only about that! And, in fact, Jesus will be doing that with John, who only has to wait... whereas Peter still has big spiritual cleaning to do?

Now John understood the high (meat) language of Jesus. He knew, apparently, that Jesus would come and "Christ-in-You" him later... especially as he wrote all those New Testament Books!

But snarky John has to let everyone know, *He understood these things first!* Because the *other disciples* broadcast abroad the stupid notion that Jesus was saying that John would live *forever (?)* until the next J*esus-in-his-own-flesh return,* which is stupid and absurd! *(Because Jesus will return spiritually in us as Christ-in-You!)* Did those disciples write any books of the Bible? Apparently not, they knew nothing of Christ-in-You, did they? *Yet John knew!* And Peter would learn later, wouldn't he? *(Will we?)*

Snarky, snarky John! Later, in the Epistles of John, he appears to be humbled... well, almost but not quite! Because in the Book of Revelation John twice falls down to worship who he thinks is the Lord, but ends up being an angel who corrects him. This happens in the first and last pages of the Book of Revelation! Which is quite humbling!

In being humble about himself, John is correcting his *earlier* snarky errors of being so excited and braggadocios about being in the know regarding Christ-in-You ops.

Lastly, John ends up mentioning the mysterious ways of meat pedagogy. Milk pedagogy usually contains rigid rules and lessons with three or four "bullet" points. Repeat and rinse... meaning the same limited stories, lines, and

95

precepts are repeated *ad nauseam*, with very little higher awareness that the milk game afoot is simplicity for simpletons and lower-consciousness souls. *Selah!*

So, before closing his Gospel book, John notes: the world would not be big enough for the long list of higher teachings Christ was bestowing on humankind. But he seems to know it is entirely unnecessary to include them all. Why?

John seemed to know that whereas in the meat pedagogy, a newbie or padawan is required to learn the first couple thousand "points of light" of meat territory... it is impossible or unprofitable to list, or explain the many more thousands of lines and precepts! Yes, we must learn, perhaps, the first thousand or so... then we are able to receive and operate in Christ-in-You... and the amazing thing is that the learning never stops, and a wise one continues to discover points of light... until the last breath!

Like Philoctetes training young Hercules in the 1997 Disney Hercules film, the Master Jedi (Phil) takes the Padawan (Hercules) from clumsy know-nothing to accomplished dragon-slayer. And Hercules does it by learning, in this case, a list of 100 points a hero needs to understand. Hercules goes from zero to hero, and *"That's the Gospel Truth,"* as the muses sang.

What am I saying here? This passage of scripture shines a very bright light on what it takes to go from milk to meat: First, slay pride. Second, learn thousands of points of light. Third, pride doesn't stay dead... it has a life of its own, for it too resurrects! Nevertheless, with sufficient requiting, rebuking, and self-discipline against religious pride...

whom God loves... can possibly be indwelt... to glory and *"greater works!"*

After all, did not Peter write a couple of great Epistles? And in Peter's writing, he confesses that ameliorating Paul (the outsider disciple) was "hard to understand" even while Peter was writing at a very high, noble, and accomplished level himself!

Bottom line, Jesus in this scene was preparing these two disciples for their massive assignments after Jesus—in the flesh—had left and gone... only to later reappear in the spirit as the dangerous Christ-in-You! *(Can seminary-church-Bible leaders now see this?)*

In That Day Teachings explain much, indeed. This explanation is not dissimilar to how ITDTs explain the Book of Job. Elihu was guiding Job and friends to higher consciousness (slaying religious pride) prerequisite to Christ-in-You indwelling and reciprocal two-way radio communications and assignments with God. At the end of Chapter 21 of John, Jesus is doing the same for obtuse Peter and following (but snarky) John. Both will later, through the expulsion of religious pride, become Christ-in-You masters.

Joseph Campbell explains Job-like stories as The Hero with a Thousand Faces. It is the price paid for ascendency?

Is this what Jesus was talking about on the last page of the Bible, where—with spiritual eyes to see and ears to hear—we are to: "Behold! I come quickly!?" Three times, Christ says it. *(Can seminary-church-Bible leaders now see this?)*

The challenge before us now is to learn and become, if possible, via the Lord's Behold: quick-come indwelling... worthy to be saluted and blessed... prepared sufficiently for

Christ-in-You indwelt living. Can seminary-church-Bible leaders ever honor "In That Day Teachings?" Is there a better time than now? Is today "In That Day?" Is today a day of denouement? Is "In That Day" the day we understand the hidden-in-plain-sight Christ-in-You process? *(Can seminary-church-Bible leaders now see this?)*

Behold, In That Day! *Can seminary-church-Bible leaders now see Christ-in-You?*

Selah. Amen.[*]

---

[*](See Col. 1:26-27; John 14:20 The Message)
(See www.inthatdayteachings.com, Book #8, Search "Fighting Leviathan")

Part IV—
Assignments/Warnings/Rights
and Responsibilities

What Are Assignments in High Country Meat Christianity?

"A lady with a lame horse told me to go heal its leg. I told her to rub a tablespoon on it. My assignment was to give her the assignment. She learned. It worked." –RWB

*W*hen you flow in God's river in the meat territory, you need to know about assignments. Your two-way radio with God must work. You must qualify as being mature enough.

A typical assignment would be to meet that Christ-in-You killer Saul, now blind, and needs a man with some God-power to restore his sight so that the born-again "Paul" can learn what needs to be learned in the milk and meat, and write pluralistic, intellectual books for the New Testament. *Just go down a street called Straight and find him!*

Of course, this is an example from the life of Paul. Milk folk know very little about how to do assignments. You can learn them as you do them. You can learn from a higher one who knows how to do them. You can know about assignments in advance. You can prepare for them. You need a working two-way radio with God. You can receive a grade from heaven afterward.

You can learn from each operation. Usually, you are helping people. The assignments are to ameliorate something or a situation. Often you will be the only meat believer present. Good work needs to occur. It is an honor and privilege to partake in an assignment.

Be careful to not add to assignments, or veer off and do other things. More about that later.[**]

---

[*](See www.inthatdayteachings.com, Book #3, Search "I Am a Man of the Cloth")

(Book #4, Search "No One Will Wail")

(Book #11, Search "(Gulp!) Shall We Dance?")

"Danger! Danger, Will Robinson!" —
Lost in Space (The Robot)

"Online dating with far-away partners is fine until somebody buys a plane ticket." –RWB

"Out of life's school of war – What does not kill me makes me stronger." – Friedrich Nietzsche

*T*o manifest Christ-in-You at significant levels requires one attaining high spiritual country territory, memes, ways, assignments, benefits, rights, and responsibilities. By now, perhaps, you have experienced more than a little bit of this. However, the danger of it all cannot be overstated!

High country visits require ruggedization of body, soul, and spirit. Feet cannot be tender, else the hike from the trailhead, over the pass, and into Beula land be too onerous. Watch the weather, lighting can kill. What are the wild beasts doing? Can you *"Learn to Return"* as the Alaskans teach newbies headed into backcountry…full of grizzly bears, some of whom kill tourists every year?

Can you *do the work* of going out and coming back in? Do you understand the process of first receiving your assignment, preparing, doing the assignment, going home from the assignment, and then understanding your grade or level of performance? Then, can you rest, recuperate, learn more, wait and do another assignment… more effectively?

And importantly, do you understand the grave consequences of *tragically adding* to an assignment by making extra visits, doing extra work, finding extra things, and diddle dawdling around unto perdition or extremely bad consequences? Simply: Go out, do the assignment, come back in. God have mercy! It is enough to do so.

And do you know how to keep the high country? This is by far the biggest problem with newbies, they get to high country and believe it their due, after all that work! Then they forget to do the disciplines, carry on in old Mesmer ways, diving gleefully into the muck of low territory… and then are surprised when the next assignment needs them, or their high country team members need them… to be a resident in the high country! And all such discover the individual is low, and it might take a long while to get back up into high country! *(Surprise, surprise, we told you so!)*

Most folk, after attaining to high country, fail to apprehend the horrific tragedy of going back to milk-level memes, ways, lines, precepts, repetitive already-known lessons, shenanigans, excuses, easy pickings, and—frankly—low-consciousness living.

Here is what happens! When a person retreats from the high country and goes into low country, Satan steals, kills, and destroys. And what is destroyed almost always includes High Teachings. They are memory-wiped, just like in the "Men in Black" movies! Yes, the memories of High Teachings are memory-wiped. It is the dangest thing to watch, as a teacher, happen to the newbies. They, inevitably, will dip their beaks deep into the old milk systems, get emotional, and Satan (actually, his minions) will gleefully steal, kill, and destroy the high calling of the individual, primarily by memory-wiping critical-to-know, and previously-hard won High Teachings.

Be warned. This is real. For a bright one, after this happens… *you should never let it happen again!* For a dumb one, they will think it is okay to do this again and again until they find they can no longer enter into the High Country of Meat.

Further, newbies to the High Country who refuse to stop going low and back into the milk realm, who force longsuffering High Country teachers to repeatedly teach the newbie *former lessons repeatedly lost* (yes, this happens)... will eventually be cut off from each other, for each other's sake! The newbie has chosen not to keep lessons or stay in the High Country, the newbie keeps letting Satan's minions in to steal, kill, and destroy... and what it means, really, in the end... is that the newbie is a threat to the High Country team members. The newbie brings too much bad into a high group, and all that ends up happening is the bad in the newbie reaches out to steal, kill, and destroy not only the newbie but the High-Country team. God never approves of this. Therefore, separation occurs by the nature of the universe. The newbie who refuses to stay in the High Country will go back to the Milk Territory, and cannot really stay in contact with the team of the High Country.

This is true not because I say it is true. It is true by the fact everyone who enters into the High Country of Meat can test and verify, "Yes, this is the way it works."

God have mercy on us all!*

---

*(See www.inthatdayteachings.com, Book #5, Search "Jabberwocky Soul Cancer")
(Book #6, Search "I Am a Monkey")
(Book #8, Search "Come and Check Me Out!")
(See Matthew 12:43-45, Luke 11:24-26. The tenant is a demon; house: a human.)

How to Maturely Understand Seasons

"In baseball, a batter gets a hit, four balls, three strikes or is beaned by the pitcher, but his time at bat is over until next at bat. He doesn't have infinite "grace" to stand at bat forever. Likewise, the seasons God gives us are to do something good. We do not get infinite "at bats." Grace can be understood as Divine Enablement, not infinite do-overs." –RWB

*I*n the milk realm, Christians barely understand the severity of God's seasons. A door God shuts, no man can open; a door God opens, no man can shut. Unfortunately, milk Christians are taught an over-emphasis on grace... the idea grace covers all sins, mistakes and rebellious actions.

Forever grace is over-emphasized in the milk realm but in the meat realm... things operate from a different point of view. Suppose you are a coach of Olympic track champions. Suppose you see and meet various high school and college track athletes. Fine and well enough. Do you treat them harshly? Do you force them into a tough training schedule? Of course not! They are simply people in the passing parade. But what about *your athletes?* Well, as an Olympic track coach, the athletes you do treat somewhat roughly, you give them a demanding workout schedule, you put them in really tough track meets, you make them do things and perform better than they thought was humanly possible. This is your job. They win.

Those in the meat realm of Christianity get to learn what God wants them to do, and they learn that "seasons" are attached to most things. There is a season to learn meat lines, precepts, truths, and operations. There is a season to do an assignment. There is a season to question your meat teacher, and for the newbie to countermand the meat teacher. There are seasons that open up, and there are seasons that close down. Why? God invented seasons, and they have timing.

Jesus mentioned how a season can work, in regards to training obtuse, rebellious, fight-you-back milk students who are taught meat from a teacher. "How many times do I forgive my *(fight-you-back)* brother?" Peter asked. "Seven times?" Jesus said in regards to teaching a newbie the meat principles, "Seventy times seven" *(i.e., 490)*. So, the teacher forgives the newbie slapping him in the face, or fighting the meat way... about 500 times... and then, after that... if the newbie keeps doing it, the newbie is "gaming" the teacher, it is a con. Drop it.

Therefore, not surprisingly... experienced teachers in the meat realm will tell the excited, agreeable newbie that the season is open for learning, but inevitably the season will be cut off, for a while, for the sake of both student and teacher. To go from darkness to light, from immature to mature, from love-mush religion to tough-as-nails religion... means the newbie will inexorably fight the teacher, and the teacher will fight the student... so both will need a cool-off period. Sometimes, sadly, these disconnects are permanent... because the newbie went past a season or past a certain measure.

Again, milk Christians learning the meat realm have a tough time figuring this out in real-time, or in actually living through it. An assignment will come for the newbie. The newbie doesn't prepare for it well enough. The assignment will be dropped. Why? The newbie blew past the season of preparation. The deal is off. Likewise, the newbie will be taught a timely but tough lesson. God ordains this lesson, because a tough real-world situation is about to come up, and learning the tough "High Country" lesson will mitigate the upcoming real-world situation, and in fact make the whole thing ameliorating. But the newbie rejects the particular High Teaching, believing there is "infinite grace" to plow on into the meat country using ineffectual milk doctrines. Well, the newbie blew past the season, then the real-world tough situation comes, and the newbie is slaughtered. Ouch! The newbie wonders why such pain? Because God still believes the newbie is going to learn. These painful lessons continue until the newbie either learns, or God sees the newbie hates the meat territory and wants to go back to the milk. So be it, then.

(See when Moses ordered Hebrews to fight and they refused but later went to fight the enemy without Moses' order and were subsequently slaughtered.)

Learn to honor seasons. Learn to honor time. God invented both. Seasons can run out. Time can run out. Do what God wants you to do in his seasons and times.[*]

---

[*](See www.inthatdayteachings.com, Book #4, Search "How to Turn a Page (into Knight!)"
(Book #4, Search "Breaking Off Adhesions")

Why Do Milk Pastors and Prophets Use Shenanigans and Neuro-Linguistic Programming Audience Control?

"What's behind the curtain, Toto?"
Answer: "Pay no attention to that man behind the curtain!"
–The Wizard of Oz, 1939 film

"Church leaders will, of this work, countermand, dismiss outright without study and 'protesteth too much' against anything beyond milk understanding. Until they see." –
RWB

*W*hen you have spiritual eyes and ears, you will see many Evangelical pastors and prophets sometimes use Neuro-Linguistic Programming (NLP) shenanigans: a) malaprop showmanship, b) stage hypnotism, c) straw-man misdirection, and d) financial suggestion. This is quite a challenging brain scramble to witness! God have mercy!

Why do they and their audiences drink this poison Kool-Aid? Because they don't know better, and they like it! Absent God's mind-meld (i.e., Christ-in-You)... this is what they do!

Restated, my people perish for lack of knowledge. *"They exchanged the truth of God for a lie, the prophets of Israel who are making things up out of their own heads and calling it 'prophesying'... aren't your sermons tissues of lies, saying 'God says...'" (Ezekiel 13:7-9 The Message)* And then, of course, there is Revelation's *"whosoever loveth and maketh a lie." (last page of the Bible)*

What is the problem with seminary-approved-and-blessed Church use of NLP? Well, it causes and locks in spiritual blindness and deafness. In addition, God doesn't abide in it. Hence, the Church's use of NLP prevaricates Christ-in-You. Restated, Church use of NLP is the singular operation that prevents, dooms, stops, and makes war against Christ-in-You, higher truth, meat territory of the spirit, and the future of God and man's restoration.

In fact, when Christ-in-You folk behold such Church NLP shenanigans… they usually leave. To do anything more, to try to correct or explain to the leaders what they are doing… will almost always result in the *"touch-not-God's-supposedly-anointed"* pastor in banishing *(if not stoning to death)* the Christ-in-You one *(as a favor to God?)*

It is time for scales to come off the eyes of milk seminaries… Then, church leaders?

Nicodemus came to Jesus at night. And he asked him questions as a true seeker. He asked Christ, how can these things of maturity be? Answer: you must be born again. He asked, go back to our mother's womb? So… you see that milk folk take things literally at first, and refuse to see things spiritually. Nothing has changed in this regard. Oh milk church leaders, will you earnestly come to "In That Day Teachings" and ask honest questions, and endeavor to partake in the meat of Christ-in-You?

How else does Christ return but as and in "Christ-in-You" before he otherwise returns? There is no better answer than Christ-in-You. There is no better time than now. Except, one must generally be high-country taught in order to salute, bless, redound, and manifest… Christ-in-You!

Will any seminaries get this and teach this? Will any church leaders? Remember, God seems to be asking 5% to wake up and learn this next, higher territory![*]

---

*(See www.inthatdayteachings.com, Book #3, See "I Killed the Monkey on My Shoulder") (Book #3, Search "To Which We Say, Hear! Hear!")

"You Can't Learn Something You Already Know..." — Country Song

"If you don't read the newspaper, you're uninformed. If you read the newspaper, you're misinformed..."—Mark Twain

*W*hat scripture revelations do In That Day Teachings (ITDTs) have? Answer: Enough... enough to take people from blind-eye, milk life to keen-eye, meat Christ-in-You!

In regards to the Book of Job, conventional wisdom teaches, "No one knows why bad things happen to good people." ITDTs say that Eliju is the book's author. Further, he is the one providing God's voice in the storm, and at the end of the book when giving instructions to Job and his friends. Young Eliju is the story's Master Jedi, enabling Job to understand that Leviathan is religious pride, and religious pride is Leviathan. Eliju takes Job, as it were, from milk to meat. *How about them apples!*

In regards to Luke's Christmas story, there is an important lesson to be filled and controlled by the Holy Spirit. There are seven individuals so filled and controlled. Why is this important? They (and one individual obedient to angels) avoid kill zones. Church congregants at Christmas could also be filled and controlled (hopefully) by the Holy Spirit, and likewise avoid kill zones the ensuing year. Being filled and controlled by the Holy Spirit means your two-way radio works pretty good with God. *How about them apples!*

In regards to Jesus' return… until he returns, the way that he returns is Christ-in-You. This must be honored in folk you see (with eyes to see and ears to hear in the spirit) and blessed. Unless you say, blessed is he or she who comes in the name (and the nature) of God then your house will remain unto you desolate of God's indwelling. (See the end of Matthew's 23rd Chapter). *How about them apples!*

In regards to Jesus being "The Word," it turns out Christ can be very picky, or judgmental to preachers and teachers *(held at a higher standard)* who use words that are essentially upside-down-opposite… or generally pejorative toward maturity and goodness. This is why bad preachers start their sermons with, "*Guys*, I have a *cool* sermon with an *impactful impartation* of *awesome stuff*, it's really *unbelievable* it's so *incredible*! *Hell-o-o-o-o-*!" God hates it when words are abused, used in antipode, or insultingly to (or against) his beloved body, the beloved ears of his body of Christ. *How about them apples!*

It turns out God doesn't like preachers using Neuro-Linguistic Programming (NLP) engaged against unbeknownst psyches *(souls)* of congregants. This means God doesn't like preachers using a) malaprop showmanship, b) stage hypnotism, c) straw-man argument misdirection, and d) subsequent financial suggestion or strong-arming of the mesmerized. So, pastors shouldn't put hands in pants when preaching and praying *(something hyper-grace leaders oft do?)* Pastors should not walk left-right to stage hypnotize audience. Pastors shouldn't start a sermon with an off-color joke, as it puts them in a dominant NLP position to an unknowing audience. It gives power, but the wrong power.

Pastors should not make straw man arguments to boldly knockdown, in preparation for financial giving mandates. Pastors should not talk high, then low and pause... which is also hypnotizing. Pastors should not build up tension from calm to manic, then repeat and rinse... which is also hypnotizing. Pastors should not go from quiet to loud, rinse and repeat... which is also hypnotizing. In short, pastors must not sin and put blinders on the audience! *How about them apples!*

Many are the profound teachings of In That Day Teachings. They need to be honored. Honor unto whom honor is due. Romans 13:7. Stupid people do not honor high things... since high principles cannot indwell them until they do honor such, they remain desolate of those high principles. Milk seminaries avoid inspecting the bad fruit of their graduates. Milk seminaries would rather teach Greek and Latin, and carefully ignore egregious NLP and stage-hypnotizing methods of their well-to-do students. This is all trash needing to be taken to the dump. Great people honor great things. Honor unto whom honor is due. *How about them apples!*

The challenge, at this point, is for your author to know when to quit. As John said at the end of his gospel, endless books *could be written.* Some must. But not every precept needs to be told. They need to be lived. Herein you have been given good fruit, many fine apples. Are you interested in destroying these apples, via brazen critique? Critique away, if you must. The real question will remain... Can you absorb this material, and with God's help, enter into the meat realm of religion and somehow strongly manifest Christ-in-You? *With these apples, can you bake a pie?**

*(See www.inthatdayteachings.com, Book #1, Search "Chapter 6") [Job: Rigid Righteous]
(Book #2, Search "Words God Hates")
(Book #3, Search "And So I Return Quickly")
(Book #3, Search "Jesus Flies Within You")
(Book #6, Search "Finding Love at Christmas One")
(Book #8, Search "Fighting Leviathan")
(Book #8, Search "The Borg for Christ!")

The Hardest Feast in the World to Actually Attend...

"Truth is not what you want it to be; it is what it is, and you must bend to its power or live a lie."—Miyamoto Musashi

"When I return, will I find faith?"—Jesus

"When hitting an attacker, teaching a disciple, or holding a baby, remain human."

—RWB

We should all be familiar with the parable of the feast, wherein the master has his servants invite well-to-do folk, who excuse themselves from attending, so the master ends up inviting the poor, except the master gets mad at a foolish man who dressed wrongly.

Let us examine this parable from the meat vs. milk perspective. Why didn't the wealthy and prosperous want to come? Because they are shamed by the master. These wealthy and prosperous, presumably, were *"living the lie,"* and were happy to invite *each other to parties.*

But the wealthy and prosperous would be called out, as Jesus did at "his" party. He said the first would be last. He said none of the rich folk cleaned and perfumed his feet! He said the rich folk all brokered for the first position at the party. In essence, he would say to them their robes are filthy, and inside they were poor, and they needed to buy the things they lack from him, spiritually! Any normal "wealthy and prosperous" crowd will, in fact, be shamed... by a true and noble master of the feast called life! *Do you understand?*

Now, the master wants to first invite the well-to-do... because learning the meat is a line upon line, precept upon precept, time-consuming task! And the well-to-do... by definition, have "the luxury" to disconnect from fast society and learn, and do and become... as the holy saints and prophets of the Bible... masters themselves. And the master (Jedi) should expect a goodly portion of the well-to-do should have figured out by now that the flashy, keep-up-with-the-Jones lifestyle of the rich and famous is vacuous!

Therefore, the well-to-do (Padawans) are the first choice to invite by the master. These folks can well afford to make the time, learn the lessons, drop the bad things, adopt the good things, walk with Jesus, travel with Jesus... and spend the years learning what it takes to learn how to be a good master. Except, none are ready. All refuse. *None believe!*

So the master decides to invite the down-trodden, who come. Now the down-trodden are a lower tier of capability group! They haven't yet learned how to make it into the higher tier of the well-to-do! Nevertheless, they can learn the meat! First, they have to plow through a lot baser things: Base anger, base prejudices, base manners, base family, base education, base everything. Except these folks sometimes work better in the meat territory (given a good guide) than the upper-crust! *Consider Jesus' fishermen disciples!*

In the story, note that one ne'er-do-well comes to the feast without a proper coat. This is apparently an on-purpose insult to the master. The master kicks this person out. This is a lesson to all. The master is NOT desperate for company, NOT desperate for disciples, NOT desperate for insults. No, the master suffers no fools.

Just because the well-to-do typically reject the master's high teachings, it doesn't mean the bottom-tier-of-society folk can bite the hand which feeds them meat!

Note that the world of milk Gospel teachers generally turn this story into a milk-mash which you can neither eat nor drink *if you know anything about the meat territory!*

How do you know if you have a milk seminary or milk preacher? By the implosions. By the pedestal stools they sit on while telling audiences they don't put themselves on pedestals. By the hands in their pants when preaching and praying. By the Neuro-Linguistic Programming (NLP). By every Mark 16:20 sign showing the reverse universal disapproval of the word going out, which is rancid milk and not healthy meat.[*]

---

[*](See Bonanza TV episode "The Saga of Squaw Charlie" i.e., Christ-in-You vs. town folk) (See 1953 Western "Shane".)
(See www.inthatdayteachings.com, Book #3, Search "To Which We Say, Hear! Hear!")
(See www.inthatdayteachings.com, Book #12, Search "What is the Blessed True North… on Preaching?")
(Book #12, Search "And… Another Hyper-Grace Scandal and Implosion?")

Part V—There You (Christ-In-You) Go/Honor to Whom Honor is Due

How are "In That Day Teachings" More Mature... than Milk-Mandarin Church?

"Via shenanigans and lack of faith, church leadership is stony-heart petrified, a strange Medusa! Look in her eyes, call out her inner demons of fear-greed-laziness and turn her rocky-cold heart into a warm, intelligent, and loving receiver of Christ-in-You?"—RWB

*T*he milk prophetic seminaries, schools, conferences, leaders, and wannabes... all pretty much say the same thing and use the same language. In short, they say, *"It's coming! It's coming! (Yawn) This time we really mean it!"* Read, then of two prophets: compared...

(This story compares differences between 1957 Chevrolet and 2007 Audi A8 sedans.)

Back in 1957, there were four prophets to the car industry: Bob, Tom, Dick, and Harry. Tom, Dick, and Harry spoke breathlessly and agitatedly as follows:

<u>In the next 50 years, cars will be...</u> Awesome, cutting edge, significant, soaked in luxury, at a new level, in sync with the environment, shaking the old order, high technology, dread champions of mileage, taken to new levels of power, called to higher transport, and raised to higher emissions purity. And the industry leaders will be shaken to the core, there will be a new vision of how to navigate, cars will change like butterflies, the world will have an incredible expectation of automobiles, people in the auto industry will find new ways to prosper, there will be a

change of rhythm of manufacturing, and it will be tumultuous but equations will equal.

People were *really* impressed with Tom, Dick, and Harry. They paid them glorious accolades because what they said was nebulous and pleasing to everyone.

However, Bob spoke with authority as follows:

In the next 50 years, carmakers must…

Stop using drum brakes on all wheels	And use discs with antilock brake systems.
Stop using iron engines, heads, and blocks	And use aluminum low-emission engines.
Stop using two valves per cylinder	And use four.
Stop using carburetors	And use fuel stratified injection.
Stop using leaded gas	And use unleaded gas.
Stop using 14" metal wheels	And use 19" aluminum.
Stop using nylon bias tires	And use radial.
Stop using steel frames and bodies	And use aluminum.
Stop using generators	And use alternators.
Stop using tube radios	And use navigation/CD/satellite radios.
Stop using just one radio speaker	And use twelve entertainment speakers.
Stop using metal dashboards	And use soft materials and airbags.
Stop using solid rear axles	And use all-wheel independent suspension.
Stop using two-speed transmissions	And use six.
Stop using the two-wheel drive	And use four.

But people *hated* listening to Bob. No one wanted to hear him or read his words. He was right, but it was not music to anyone's itching ears since it involved hard, actual change.

In 2007, a fellow by the name of Robert Winkler Burke said the modern media church which broadcasts its message through the United States and by satellite around the world must...

Stop preaching the lie of the rapture
And preach God's overwhelming scourge.

Stop waiting for God to manifest Himself
And preach we *must* manifest God Himself.

Stop preaching dispensational fear
And preach overcoming peace.

Stop dreading a governmental mark of 666
And preach it is a mark of spirit, soul, body.

Stop preaching in outrageously evil spirits
And worship God in spirit and truth.

Stop modeling greed and self-interest
And be non-profit leaders of non-profits.

Stop insisting God's rules are inviolate
And preach God delights in breaking rules.

Stop extorting and demanding tithes
And preach Jesus criticized tithing people.

Stop preaching eternal security
And preach only God guarantees absolution.

Stop preaching foreign affairs intrigue
And preach personal overcoming of evil.

Stop purchasing costly jets with donations	And travel with commoners and be humble.
Stop preaching fear of a Euro-antichrist	And be sure not to be of any ungodly spirit.
Stop pandering to spirits of envy of success	And preach the fear of God and His scourging.
Stop selling each other's evil books	And promote listening to the spoken Bible.
Stop idolizing easy-on-the-ears "prophets"	And allow rebuking prophets to speak the truth.
Stop praying for an uncorrected revival	And repent of being unworthy of revival.
Stop preaching six-day creationism	And admit the earth is as old as science says.
Stop cursing who comes in God's nature	And bless those who come in God's nature.
Stop fighting the ACLU's efforts	And fight the Church's efforts to deny God.
Stop fighting the full baptism of the Spirit	And encourage the full baptism of the Spirit.
Stop fighting the full baptism of the Fire	And encourage the full baptism of the Fire.
Stop evil controlling techniques in crowds	And repent massively of using evil control.
Stop preaching only "about" Jesus	And manifest His essence so others learn.

And… for an update, please compare a 1967 Plymouth GTX with a 2019 Mercedes Benz E43. Search the internet and compare specifications.

The point here is that milk prophets use nebulous, flowery language to herald many things they don't know will come about.

Real prophets (of the meat territory) can specifically describe what's wrong with the existing milk church, and how to do the right thing.

Restated, milk prophets are necessarily unspecific and wordy. Meat prophets speak of specific egregious actions that must stop and be repented of, and they speak of what the right thing to do subsequently is. Milk prophets entertain and fall usually under the spiritual covering of uncorrectable church pastors. Meat prophets refuse to allow themselves to come under the cover of uncorrectable church pastors because meat prophets are trying to correct the perdition of uncorrectable church pastors, get them to publicly repent, and then do the correct thing.

In sum, by now you can see milk prophets have sort of a cheap con, they keep saying, "It's coming, coming," but what is coming is a correction to church leaders, and milk prophets who aren't mature enough to give them that message. Meat prophets are mature enough, but immature pastors insist milk prophets come under their corrupted covering, a thing true prophets cannot allow. *(Is this true for Christian publishing, as well?)*

The most mature movies will admit as to how people are corrupt, but love rules and reigns anyway. See the *Paper Moon* (1973) film, where all are corrupt but very loveable...

and the best folk are loving each other anyway. God have mercy!*

---

*(See www.inthatdayteachings.com, Book #3, Search "There Must be a Better Shibboleth")
(Book #3, Search "Who am I to tell Them?")
(Book #9, Search "Mexican Standoff, Described In That Day")
(Book #11, Search "Say We Made Smoking-Hot, Passionate Love")
(Book #12, Search "I Sit on an Unasked-for Throne of Skulls")

Do "In That Day Teachings" Enable High Denouement?

"Understand the aggregate of In That Day Teachings and behold Christ-in-You." –RWB

*W*hat are "In That Day Teachings" (ITDTs) designed to do? Answer: For those called to it, ITDTs are designed to help such manifest Christ-in-You at high levels unto effectual eyes and ears of the Spirit, to enable ameliorating assignments from heaven, to be synchronized and congruent with God and man with all that is good while also being distanced in measured enmity with all that is bad.

This *meat-and-not-milk territory* of Christianity tends to percolate marvelously with extraordinary powers of healing energy, flowing-with-the-universe "groaning" for the Christ-in-You revealing thereof, words of wisdom, avoidance of kill zones, functional two-way radios with God, finding-flowing-flourishing in God's invisible rivers of life, deep spirit unto deep spirit communication with others, and so on and so forth. Frankly speaking, ITDTs have no simple, salable premise. They are a sword like no other.

In addition, this "restoration of all things" territory of the Spirit almost always causes milk believers to attack the ascendant one, while the ascendant one takes all such abuse praying for *red-pill-awakening-moments* for the world's sleeping milk seminaries, milk Christian leadership, milk Christian conferences, milk evangelism, and milk folk.

God wants us to be more fully realized human beings.

Interestingly, manifestations of Christ-in-You power in a mature individual are more or less resident and don't need any "huffing and puffing" to perform. It is instant on, not a four-hour church service of soulish baloney build up. The woman with the issue of blood simply touched Jesus' hem of the garment, and virtue healing power flowed out. At perhaps lesser levels, so it is with meat Christians indwelt of Christ-in-You. They are mostly always, "On." Their power is continuous. Frankly, they have to hide or camouflage it.

The touch of a meat-level Christ-in-You one calms the crying baby (storm). To be given their back is a dread. If their face shines upon you, you are energized. Virtue energy flows from the palms of their hands. Their whole body is an antenna for energy, easily obtaining this invisible energy, easily giving it to others… while most others in the world only can detect something in these God-charged individuals which must be disdained and put down. The milk seminaries, the milk church leaders and the milk Bible study groups miss God by a mile because they hate the idea that if they were purer, they could see God… in such as us, the persecuted ones indwelt by Christ-in-You, as Paul foretold.

In this day of denouement, God wants 5% of milk ones to enter into the steak territory of Christ-in-You manifestation. The exigencies of the world require it. The time that the world is now in, requires it. Humans know it and feel it. Until now, they haven't really had a manual or text whereby they can understand the process.

Dear reader, enjoy the journey! It is worth the cost! It is, indeed, good!*

*(See www.inthatdayteachings.com, Book #4, Search "Spirited Away")

(Book #4, Search "On Trial: The Mined and Blind")

(Book #4, Search "Saga of the Seeker")

(Book #8, Search "If Not Now, When Shall Self-Interest Church be Exposed?")

"If You Are So Smart, how Come You Ain't Rich?" Country Saying

"Bring a gift to first meetings with higher folk. Honor unto whom honor is due."—RWB

*I*n regards to In That Day Teachings (ITDTs), the bulk of the effort is to enrich people spiritually, to be controlled and not just filled with the Spirit. This, the teachings do.

John wrote, "I would that you prosper *(in the world like patriarchs Abraham, Joseph, Moses, David)* even as your soul prospers *(i.e., Christ-in-You!)*"

We might find it hard to believe and even harder to actually live out... but God and heaven are keenly interested first in our true spiritual growth from milk to meat while, at the same time, testing us as to how long we can hold out... growing spiritually and not yet financially!

Restated, come all ye who seek true spiritual wealth! But at the same time, this *tour de force* work makes no guarantees of financial rewards!

However, one wealth is supposed to follow the other wealth. The carnal world does things backward. Most people find it easier to first get wealthy with money, fame, and power... and then are surprised by fear of implosion and then implosion. But the ITDTs world first gives you spiritual enrichment... a thorough and sufficient-for-the-task operation going from milk to meat, from being desolate-of-Christ... to being indwelt of Christ-in-You at various levels.

In That Day Teachings are congruent with Scottish Common Sense Philosophy which guided the founding fathers of the US. To gain financial wealth, common sense says you must provide a good product, service, or return on investment for customers.

Dumbed-down milk church leaders say that if you give them donations, God will bless you financially. Really? *Has this been grossly overemphasized?*

God wants us to be smart enough to see when a Prosperity Preacher offers you a thousand-fold return from God by you giving the preacher a thousand dollars... meaning the conman is telling you you'll get a million dollars (from God) by giving the preacher (conman) a thousand dollars... God wants you to be smart enough to laugh and walk away. To be able to do so consistently is to be very rich in spirit, and financially, you can perhaps later become rich by humbly providing a good product, service, or return on investment to customers.

You see in this example, the conman preacher has, in essence, one real contract with you. That contract says you give him $1,000 in return or in consideration of nothing from him... nothing except a fake contract #2 between you and God saying that God will give you a 1,000-fold return, or $1 million! But contract #2 is fake, or an illusion, or imaginary. There is no contract #2. You were duped, that's all. You only have contract #1, in which you give $1,000 to the conman preacher, and he gives you a contract between you and another party whom he cannot be the guarantor. However, it is a clever sham!

It's like me getting $1,000 from a home-owner for a contract, to replace the front door, so I give the rube homeowner a contract between the homeowner and Joe's Front Door Service. But I never met this Joe. With my contract #1 between myself and the homeowner, take the money and run providing only contract #2! It is bogus!

In That Day Teachings are a good tree, making good, spiritual fruit, whereas milk prosperity preaching (selling subtext greed) is a tree making inedible fruit. Ditto for rapture preaching (selling subtext fear) and ditto for emergent preaching (selling subtext laziness). In That Day Teachings help a person to think. Thinking about thinking aids thinking. Eventually, with the right doctrine, mind-melds begin to happen with Jesus, and then... behold, for eyes to see and ears to hear spiritually... quickly comes Christ-in-You!

See the last page of the Bible where Jesus three times says, "Behold, I come quickly!"[*]

---

[*](See www.inthatdayteachings, Book #3, Search "And So I Return Quickly")
(Book #4, Search "I Bought the Broadcasters' Philosopher's Stone")

"Okay Houston, We've Had a Problem Here." — *Apollo 13 Astronaut Jack Swigert Jr*

"In any troubled situation, the answer usually is to do the mature thing. However, people in a troubled situation rarely want to do the mature thing." –RWB

Consider Assignments: A - B - C - D - E - F - G

*I*f God can't get you *(once you are qualified as a meat Christian can-do person)* to understand a peculiar high-country assignment is to go and do "***F***," then under certain extreme conditions, God will get you to move and do "***D***," because it's close to "***E***." *See what is going on here? From your viewpoint: chaos. But from God's viewpoint, you are getting closer, as it were, to pinning the tail on the donkey.*

Once you are doing the "***D***" thing (because it is closer to "***E***") then God will shut down "***D***" and have you move to nearby "***E***" (because it is even closer to "***F***.") Then God will shut down the "***E***" operation because now you're going to do "***F***," and "***F***" gets done. *This whole thing is very, very messy and seemingly not only dystopian but wildly pricey.*

Restated, important assignments from God sometimes absolutely need to be done. And God will find a way that they get done, even if his servants can't go a direct route. (See the life of patriarch Joseph. *What a wild and pricey assignment that was!*)

Look at the 1992 Unforgiven film about 1881 Wyoming. Assassins were hired to kill some bad cowboys. It turns out later, the cowboys targeted really weren't bad operators... rather it was the sheriff and the sheriff's henchmen who were the bad operators needing removal from the town of Big Whisky. The assassin Will Munny (played by Clint Eastwood) ends up doing the removing, but it is a wild and pricey ride.

In That Day Teachings are entirely spiritual, of course, but the ride can still be wild.

Do not take what happens to you personally. A good day for you is just a day. A bad day for you is just a day. No need to have an emotional rollercoaster ride. In whatever you do, remain human. When shooting a rifle, remain human. When changing a baby's diaper, remain human. When stopping a crime, remain human. When starting a revolution, remain human. Remain kind. Be a good human. Let right be done. Shake hands with better. Hello, Christ-in-You.

In the 1959 movie 'Ben Hur,' Potius Pilate says to Hur regarding bad leader Messala, "What he did has had its way with him. Where there is greatness, great government or power, even great feeling or compassion; error also is great. We progress and mature by fault."

All of the creation groans for the revealing of Christ-in-You... in humans. And when we fail, as George Harrison wrote, "With every mistake... surely, we must be learning." *Selah.*[*]

---

[*](See lyrics of and listen to The Beatles' "While My Guitar Gently Weeps")

(See www.inthatdayteachings.com, Book #3, Search "I am a Man of the Cloth")

(Book #4, Search "No One Will Wail")

Why Rebel Against Tyranny
Of Progressive Enslavement?

"People don't like to be meddled with. We are presently engaged in an epic battle between them that do like to meddle others and them who pledge allegiance to not bother others. Who do you think will win?" –RWB

*I*n the future, it will be thought archaic that a wicked philosophy made of, for and by tyrants... the evil Progressive brain-enslaving philosophy of, "Morals are, heh heh, relative," and, "No proposition can be proved true, SUCKERS!" was forced upon innocent souls for a hundred plus years of evil progressivism. This, in a hundred years, will be considered archaic.

Certain people in European leadership in 1865 were aghast that slavery was no longer possible in chains, so they invented a better way of enslaving people by simply abusing the psyches of citizens, and making them defective. The process is called progressivism. The point is to tie up people with rigid rules while enabling the same leaders to become exclusively, fantastically and exquisitely rich, powerful, and self-elevated.

Why? If leaders weren't automatically exempt from rigid rules, then guns of bandits would point skyward when they say, "Everybody, put your hands up!" (*Explanation: bandits keep guns pointed at victims, not hands up in the air. Or, Congressmen pass laws exempting themselves from taxes or penalties applied to citizens.*)

The answer is 1776—tragic liberty. Its adherents pledge mutual allegiance to freedom's self-restraint and stopping them without within.

Unfortunately, some church and seminary leaders became masters of mental shenanigans, instead of following the example of Mark Twain, who was always believing that an American thinks for himself. Twain was always explaining how cons work!

"It's easier to fool people than to convince them that they have been fooled."—Mark Twain

Likewise, it is difficult for Q or Qanon to convince the US public they have been fooled by a corrupt media, government, business, entertainment, and Deep State complex. Likewise, it is very difficult to convince seminary, church, and Bible study leaders they have been fooled into a low consciousness level of absurd repetition avoiding Christ-in-You manifestation and synchronicity with God... rather than accept the high teachings of ITDTs which would usher in Christ-in-You manifestation and oneness with the mind of God!

Church Immaturities:

25 Theses for Christian Church Leaders!

Where in We Must Either Laugh, Cry or Change

By Robert Winkler Burke, copyright 2005
Book #1, "In That Day Teachings"
Reno, Nevada USA
www.inthatdayteachings.com

Praying for Uncorrected Revival vs. Repenting of the Wrong Doctrine...

John the Baptist said to repent. Jesus said to repent. And their sharpest words were directed against the religious leaders of the day. But the religious leaders of *today* say that they, *themselves*, have nothing much to repent about. Instead, they call for revival for an unrepentant, uncorrected Church. American preachers now find revival chiefly in third-world countries who are hearing the mega ministry spiel for the first time. But in America, faith-movement leaders are finding very little new manna. In the modern nations, who have heard the faith message for many years, revival waits. Like Mark Twain's Huckleberry Finn, we "got to decide, forever, betwixt two things." The Church either must massively repent regarding the wrong doctrine or pray giddily for heavenly affirmation for an uncorrected Church's revival. The Church tells us it is righteous, blessed, and needing only our money. To believe anything else is, well, to be wrong, damnably so. But perhaps we can help this Church self-enslaved to the wrong doctrine escape its shackles of deception. Perhaps we can say, with irony as did Huck when he went against his religious upbringing and helped his friend Jim escape slavery, "All right, then, I'll go to hell."[*]

---

[*](See www.inthatdayteachings.com, Book #4, Search "Philosopher's Stone")
(See Book #7, Search "The Church of Emergent Gobbledygook")

"Do They Provoke Me to Anger? Saith The Lord..."
—Jeremiah 7:19a

"How many years can some people exist, before they're allowed to be free?
How many times can a man turn his head, and pretend that he just doesn't see?
The answer, my friend, is blowin' in the wind..."—Bob Dylan

"This is the way of an adulterous woman: she eats, and wipes her mouth, and [brazenly] says, 'I have done no wrong.'"—Proverbs 30:20 NASB

Cowgirl to Cowboy, "When are you going to grow up?" Cowboy, "I'm getting tired of that kind of talk!" Cowgirl, "Then, grow up!"—1952 film High Noon

*T*hey *(Church seminaries, leaders and publishers)* busted Church. In That Day Teachings fix Church. They reject In That Day Teachings. God says to whom, "Grow up?"

If... In That Day Teachings were not true about the meat realm... why then does milk church rely on audience manipulation shenanigans? Why the cornucopia of NLP?

Milk church leaders pretend they know not what spirit they are of. They often provide the text of the Bible with a subtext emotion (underlying spirit) of greed, fear, laziness, or worse. This is how they sell, respectively, give-to-get-cons, end-times-ink-blot-imaginings and seeker-friendly-emergent-hyper-grace gobbledygook via bad emotions sold brazenly. *Spiritually, is this like the brazen woman of Proverbs 30:20?*

Milk seminary leaders pretend their students don't do this after learning Greek and Hebrew and other traditions that make blind people from highest seminary president, down to deceiving pastor at a church, down to the poor soul who sweeps the dust between pews.

It is not easy to reject In That Day Teachings, but seminary leaders, church leaders, and Christian publishers do their best to make it look easy.

When Christian leaders have only faith in audience manipulation techniques and not finding higher truths... then they tend to use Neuro-Linguistic Programming (NLP) which then—in the spirit of things—horrifically blinds leaders and followers alike! How they love a) malaprop showmanship, b) stage hypnotism, c) straw man argument knock-downs and, d) financial strong-arming (once the listeners are unbeknownst manipulated into defenseless low-consciousness). *Oh, the horror! Oh, the humanity!*

By insisting that God cannot usher into the modern world a higher-consciousness of non-manipulative Christianity... church leaders in seminary, pulpit, and publishing arenas attempt to make sanity having none effect.

Of course, when supercilious leaders of Christianity reject sanity, the opposite redounds back onto them. It is how God made the universe. If you bless a Christ-in-You indwelt one, it tends to redound back to you. By being humble, you can become a vessel hosting the world's most precious and sanest gift: Christ-in-You!

However, if leaders in the Christian seminary, pulpit, and publishing want to reject In That Day Teachings, what do they get? What did Jeremiah write regarding this principle? Jeremiah wrote in chapter 7, verse 19, *"Do they provoke me to anger? Saith the LORD: do they not provoke themselves to the confusion of their own faces?"*

What a day of denouement! Church and State *were* wrapped up in deception and being deceived. The State is *now* "draining the swamp." The State is, therefore, causing "The Great Awakening" and going "From Darkness to Light." What is Church doing? *(See Qanon.)*

Shall a false revival occur wherein new believers are funneled into swamp churches of deceiving and deception? Shall a revival of new believers go to churches that create unbeknownst low consciousness in order to abscond funds of new believers? Didn't this previously make congregants into very poor citizens whom the politicians sheared mercilessly?

If the State is in the glorious process of repairing itself, wouldn't God have made clear a similar path of redemption for milk church? Would that path be In That Day Teachings? Can Christian leaders in seminary, church, and publishing utterly reject In That Day Teachings *and* stop their use of bad spirits to extract funds from believers they have reduced consciousness to horrific, almost-slave-like conditions?

In That Day Teachings explain the typical enmity a shenanigan pastor has for his or her duped congregants. Since apparently this pastor's seminary didn't explain or have as a witness the meat territory of Christ-in-You... this pastor can only *diss*, like a parasite, the host body. This explains why pastors address congregants as "guys" and not "beloved," why pastors tell malaprop showmanship jokes, then launch into NLP's Stage (left-right-walk) hypnotism, straw man knockdown misdirection and resultant financial extraction from the mesmerized audience. As the Muses sang in the 1997 Disney Hercules film... where villain Hades lived among the dead in the underworld, ***"Hades thought the dead were dull and uncouth... and that's the Gospel Truth!"*** Indeed, High Teachings explain much!

One thing is certain: *As a man thinks, so he is.* Christian leaders in seminary, church, and publishing have a choice:

same-old, same-old… or restoration to sanity, on a parallel basis to what the State is already doing. Does milk church want to reject doctrine which enables Christ-in-You maturity? Or would milk church leaders rather keep at the deceptive low-consciousness meals force-fed its inmates?

These leaders have put themselves into a painful "Valley of Decision." The choice seems easy: Keep mental enslavement, or repent and provide Christ-in-You amelioration. One way or the other, God will have his way. But Christian leaders are rather rigid-righteous and stubborn, aren't they? Until denouement, we can tell them the old Navajo saying: *"Think what you want, live with your thoughts."*

"Do They not Provoke Themselves
to the Confusion of Their Own
Faces?"
— Jeremiah 7:19b

Sadly, modern Evangelical church seminary, Church, and Bible study leaders oft believe shenanigans are the future of Christianity, and not the meat of Christ-in-You mind-melding with the most intelligent mind in the universe, where all shenanigans are seen by the eyes as foolish blinding and all shenanigans are heard by the ears and rejected as antipodal-to-indwelling. Until such denouement, sub-taught prophets will continue to gleefully entertain congregants unto perdition… without hope of any elevation unto high country teachings, scourging and overcoming to the better manifestation of the indwelt Christ-in-You? Consider then, that Christ-in-You seems to suffer no fools.

Where is the honest reporting of this disaster? Where is the weeping, wailing and howling among "red-pilled" leaders of seminary, church, and Bible study? All: Absent without leave, AWOL. AWOL unto permanent perdition, until… until people actually see what they are doing? This is the day of denouement; these then are the teachings of "In That Day." *(See James 5:1-11, The Message.)*

Who has heard the New Jersey radio broadcast of the airship Hindenburg Disaster of 1937?

"It's practically standing still now. They've dropped ropes out of the nose of the ship, and they've been taken ahold of down on the field by a number of men. It's starting to rain again; it's—the rain has slacked up a little bit. The back motors of the ship are just holding it just, just enough to keep it from—It burst into flames!

"Get this, Charlie! Get this, Charlie! It's fire—and it's crashing! It's crashing terrible! Oh, my, get out of the way, please! It's burning and bursting into flames, and the—and it's falling on the mooring mast and all the folks agree that this is terrible, this is one of the worst catastrophes in the world. [Indecipherable words(s)] It's, it's... it's the flames, oh, four-or-five hundred feet into the sky and it... it's a terrific crash ladies and gentlemen. It's smoke, and it's flames now... and the frame is crashing to the ground, not quite to the mooring mast. <u>Oh, the humanity</u>... and all the passengers screaming around here. I told you, I can't even talk to people whose friends are on there. Ah! Its... it's... it's... o—ohhh! I... I can't talk, ladies and gentlemen. Honest, it's just lying there, a mass of smoking wreckage. Ah! And everybody can hardly breathe and talk, and the screaming. Lady, I... I'm sorry. Honest: I... I can hardly breathe.

"I... I'm going to step inside where I cannot see it. Charlie, that's terrible. Ah, ah ... I can't. I, listen, folks, I... I'm gonna have to stop for a minute because I've lost my

voice. This is the worst thing I've ever witnessed."—
Herbert Morrison, radio journalist. [*]

[*](See www.inthatdayteachings.com, Book #3, Search "To Which
We Say, Hear, Hear!")
(Book #4, Search "The Most Incomplete Story Ever Told")
(Book #6, Search "Tie Me Up Until Denouement!")
(Book #6, Search "In That Day Unbound")
(Book #8, Search "American Revival: Jets Away!")

Conclusions

What About the Future?

Above all, a good heaven.
Beneath all, a good foundation,
In all, a good God.

Jesus wants to strongly manifest in every man, woman, and child possible. But it takes maturity beyond milk. Apostle Paul called it the Mystery of God. He called it meat. He called it Christ-in-You. Read Col. 1: 26-27.

Honor Christ-in-You in others, and perhaps Christ-in-You can redound. I—*or should I say, we*—hope Christ-in-You redounds to all, and all will be synchronized with good according to God's plan... and simultaneously all will be conflicted or distanced from bad, in each case according to God's measure.

This then, as this book ameliorates, is how—*until Jesus returns*—Jesus returns. Enjoy the indwelt High Country, for truly... it is good! Man, God: one.

Yet given truth and right spirit,
    The good ship Christianity can turn around,
Imbued quickly at once at last,
    God lives in man, man lives in God unbound![*]

---

[*](See www.inthatdayteachings.com, Study, study, study and redound unto Christ-in-You!)
(See www.inthatdayteachings.com, Book #6, Search "In That Day Unbound")

"It's the Same Old Tune... Are You Sure Hank Done It This Way?"
— Waylon Jennings

*F*rom "In That Day Teachings" magnum opus, Book #1...

25 Theses for Christian Church Leaders!

Wherein We Must Either Laugh, Cry, or Change

By Robert Winkler Burke, copyright 2005
Book #1, "In That Day Teachings"
Reno, Nevada USA
www.inthatdayteachings.com

Unrighteous Capitulation vs. the Sword of Truth and Spirit...

Country western singer Waylon Jennings wrote, *"Lord, it's the same old tune, fiddle and guitar. Where do we take it from here?... It's been the same way for years. We need a change."* Many television preachers teach rule-based tithing, rapture, eternal security, dispensational dogma, the imminent return of Just-Fix-Everything-Instantly-Jesus (their *own miscreant selves excluded*, of course!) and that the *only* prophet is an *entertaining* one. Such prophets could not get even a dog that wet the carpet to show remorse. Yet the Church itself is neither housebroken nor repentant enough for God to indwell at sufficient levels. In truth, there is no rapture, no eternal security and Jesus comes quickly in the prepared-for-Him-inside now. Giving must be Rhema-based, not percentage rule-based. The Church's end-times dispensational doctrine is a colossally wrong misdirection and poorly prepares the Church, much less the world, for tomorrow's troubles. Tribulations come with an opportunity to be sanctified because hard circumstances penetrate a soul's stupor. Only when the Church teaches the disciplines required to worship God in spirit and truth and then hear and obey Christ's Rhema voice will the Church be equal to tomorrow's emergencies, opportunities, *and* potential revivals. TV preachers rake in millions of dollars in sales by pandering fear, greed, and giddiness to sheep worldwide. This, despite occasional rebel critics who, to paraphrase Jennings, ask, *"Are you sure Christ done it this way?"* Truly, the Church has missed it by a mile. Ministries will have to massively repent of wickedly hanging on to wrong doctrines, which make them unable to manifest Christ themselves, and for their brazen audacity in hawking their worldly antichrist opinions like voracious whores. Why should God's people buy Satan's doctrines *from the Church*? Church leaders, wash the inside of the cup. Church leaders, die to self. Church leaders, stop extracting dollars un-righteously. Church leaders, stop flailing at the world with a scabbard of puerile doctrines and pick up Christ's two-edged sword of spirit and truth. And use that sword against your wrong beliefs and your wrong spirits. And then publicly repent of your misdeeds of proclaiming truth that was not truth and being of a spirit that was not of God. The world will see you become more and more like God's very truth and even like God's very spirit. *And then, verily, verily* *the Lord God Almighty says unto you, you will see true revival.*[*]

Amen, Amen, and Amen.

"I Have Something to Say, and No One to Say It to."
— Ted Nottingham

Milk Seminary theologians and leaders seem to say, "You have everything to learn (about milk) from us, and we have nothing to learn from you (about meat) in this lifetime (of never manifesting Christ-in-You, which is why we give our backs to manifestations of Him)?"

"When I return, will I find faith?"—Jesus

"None are so blind as those who will not see."—Common Saying.

"It is difficult to get a man to understand something when his salary depends upon his not understanding it!"—Upton Sinclair

"Truth is not what you want it to be; it is what it is, and you must bend to its power or live a lie."—Miyamoto Mushashi

"There are a thousand hacking at the branches of evil to one who is striking at the root."—Henry D. Thoreau

*U*ntil the milk, and therefore blind, seminaries, church leaders and Bible study groups can see and hear spiritually, In That Day Teachings are "all dressed up with nowhere to go." Why? Because when it comes to (meat-level) eyes to see and ears to hear spiritually, only God can open the spiritual doors of a person's (milk-insolent) soul, apparently.

Restated: We hold these In That Day Teachings to be self-evidently true, high teachings of Christ-in-You, "meat manifesting" territory. *Milk believers won't see, hear, or believe this until God opens a spiritual door for them.*

In addition, unless you say blessed is he or she who comes in the name and the nature of the Lord, or Christ-in-You, your spiritual houses will remain unto you desolate of God's spiritual manifestation. *(See Matthew 23:38-39.)* The pure in heart, then, really are blessed because they shall see God in others, salute and bless it, and then God redounds back into their humble spirits. *(Milk people hate this process, meat people love it!)*

Hence, we have been stuck for 2,000 years, as it were, in a Mexican standoff. Jesus wants to manifest at a high percentage in every man, woman, and child possible… but milk church prevaricates (and prevents at all times) it with all of its might, as a favor to God!

This, then, is what is happening until Jesus returns. Restated, until Jesus returns, Jesus returns in Christ-in-You and marvelously synchronizes all good with good while simultaneously distancing the good from bad in wise measure. Is this the 1776 tragic liberty wherein we pledge mutual allegiance to freedom's self-restraint and stopping them without within? *(See Gettysburg Address, See Lincoln's Lyceum Speech.)*

It is no wonder that all along, In That Day Teachings predicted God would have the State restore itself before Church, because with talk radio for 30 years pioneering the restoration of the State, this became the order: first, State repairs itself, then later, Church.

Note that 500 years after Martin Luther posted his 95 Theses on the Wittenberg Door, Q or Qanon started posting on the internet on October 28, 2017. These postings describe "the plan" to restore the rule of law and the US Constitution to "we, the people." It involves "the calm before the storm," "the storm," "the great awakening," "trust(ing) the plan," "future proves the past," "use logic," "enlarge your thinking," to be a thinking patriot, "sheep no more" wherein the US goes "from darkness to light."

In short, Q Patriots learn to ascend above the milk to the meat territory of higher awareness. "Where We Go One, We Go All!" *(WWG1WGA)*

"The history of liberty," Hillsdale College president Edmund Fairfield said in 1853, "is the history of intelligence. Ignorance is prerequisite to slavery: the more ignorance, the more slavery."—*from the book "Liberty and Learning" by Larry P. Arnn*

Behold then, a restoration of all things. It is therefore hoped at this time seminary and church leaders can see the magnum opus, Rosetta Stone of higher understanding (i.e., meat pedagogy) of Christ-in-You... provided just in time, via In That Day Teachings... for you, dear reader.—Amen[*]

[*](See www.inthatdayteachings.com, Book #3, Search "I am a Man of the Cloth")

(Book #3, Search "To Which We Say, Hear! Hear!")

(Book #6, Search "Tie Me Up Until Denouement!")

(Book #10, Search "Leaving Breadcrumb Trails for Agernon")

(Book #8, Search "Ding Dong! The Dumbed-Down Church")

(Book #8, Search "Fighting Leviathan")

(Book #10, Search "Calling All Statesmen!")

(Book #9, Search "So Far, No Detective Detection!")

(See www.inthatdayteachings.com, Book #8, Search "Have the Lions of Truth Awoken?")

(Book #5, Search "Who Uses Useful Idiots?")

(Book #9, Search "Mexican Standoff")

(Book #8, Search "The Borg for Christ")

(Book #6, Search "In That Day Unbound")

"When a Crime Goes Unpunished, the World Is Unbalanced, when a Wrong is Unavenged, the Heavens Look Down on Us in Shame."

— 2013 Film "47 Ronin"

"What does 'The wolf shall lay down with the lamb' mean? It references great days of denouement when right smart Christ-in-You souls organize society such that the quicker-faster-smarter don't subjugate the slower-dumber among us. July 4, 1776, was a good start, but progressive masterminds trumped Lincoln's fight against slavery, to mentally put us in evil, unbeknownst slavery of unchanging Weltanschauung." –RWB

"Trust the plan." –Q and Q+

*C*ertain families for over 100 years have set up a system of ill-gotten income by forcing nations to give the right to print or create the currency of each nation away from each nation's treasury and to themselves, these families.

These families force a nation, when needing currency, to sell bonds to these families who in a fashion create the funds to purchase these bonds out of nothing. The families, of course, buy these bonds at discount... expecting to be repaid in full face value (pretend: 6%?) When the government later taxes citizens, they pay these families the face value of the bonds... i.e., 100% of the face value. These families then destroy the currency principal (94% of the money received) but keep for themselves a cool 6%... in this example. *(Who knows the interest or dollar amounts?)* Over time, these families have infinite cash with which to purchase the left and right leaders of each nation.

Hence, much has been fake: these families might be puppet masters who control via skullduggery, blackmail (control files) or corruption's purchase. These families might have bought off leaders of politics, media, entertainment, medical, Church *(Orthodox and Evangelical)*, and business. So, the world is trapped in moronic slavery until each nation takes back the right to print currency from these families.

The plan from Q or Qanon is designed, one supposes, to restructure these private reserves so that these families no longer get infinite money to corrupt the world. We wish no violence upon these families, but it is cause for great reflection that the Church didn't stop the State from becoming so corrupted, neither did the Church cause a revival in State to uncorrupt itself. Nay, rather, it is the US Military and its intelligence group which received a plan of God or created a plan of God… to restore liberty, rule of law, and the US Constitution unto its people.

Hence, <u>it is hoped that the Church will weep, wail and howl in repentance</u> that for a long century or more… the Church participated in *shenaniganry* to control the masses, instead of removing shenanigans from itself and the masses. *(Selah.)* Seminary and church leaders apparently didn't have the faith or mind to re-pioneer the correct path. *(The US Military did.)* Church leaders seemed quite happy to blind and deafen congregants… *as the unbeknownst blind leading the blind into a ditch?* Otherwise, Church would have led, not been behind, the God-blessed Qanon-Trump-US-Military movement to restore liberty to first the US and later, the world.

Well, it apparently had to be this way. And "In That Day Teachings" are here for such a time as this, a day of mass denouement, biblically called in both Old and New Testaments: *"In That Day."*

First, the Church must repent massively for sticking to mesmerizing milk shenanigans, a rancid milk gone way past its due date! This sad activity powerfully disconnected the prophetic and every other branch of Church doings from God the Father, Son, and Holy Spirit. *Almost all became blind to mass global enslavement.*

After repentance, the Church must get out bad doctrines and put in good doctrines. This will repair, on a worldwide basis, the two-way radios built into each human to communicate quietly and effectually with our planet's Maker.

At that time, the good of God will be more synchronized and harmonized in effective congruence with good, heaven, and God. Likewise, this same group will then be also synchronized and harmonized in effective congruence to be distanced in proper, guided and measured discord against all that is bad, hellish, and evil.

Welcome, then, to "In That Day Teachings." They are a sword like no other! As a whole, the teachings are an epic Rosetta Stone of understanding, a tour de force, a magnum opus, a necessary creation to bridge from milk Christianity to Meat Christ-in-You manifestation in all heavenly maturity!

Church now can live up to its potential, stop obfuscating and obviating God-indwelling, understand how Christ returns for eyes to see and ears to hear spiritually… before and until Christ later at some point literally returns in his literal body, and instead enable the Mystery of God Paul knew, discussed and lived so well… the *Behold (with humble, spiritual eyes and ears), I come quickly… **Christ-in-You!***

He which testifies to these things says, Surely, I come quickly! Amen. [God have mercy!] Even so, come, Lord Jesus.—Revelation 22:20[*]

Amen.

---

[*](See www.inthatdayteachings.com, Book#11, Search "Clipped-Wing Warriors")

(Book #12, Search "One Last Chance?")

(See www.qanon.pub, Search "Owned and Controlled Banks")

In That Day Teachings

Jesus Returns While Rome Burns
How Jesus Manifests in Surprised Souls

Tough Ancient Paths Beyond Christian Escapist Messages—The In That Day Teachings of Robert Winkler Burke of Reno, Nevada excoriate broadcast Christianity's triune escapology doctrines of 1) escape by rapture, 2) the imminent return fixing all things but escapists, and 3) escape from responsibility eternally via eternal security. He says these doctrines are unbiblical imaginings caused by weak and wishful minds. He says spiritual scourging, overcoming, and God-indwelling are the paramount doctrinal positions supported by the Bible. Burke does not deny that Christ will return, he simply denies the escapology doctrines obfuscating Christ's return. Further, Burke says escapology—by definition—has little truth in its dispensational future scenarios, but that In That Day Teachings' prophetic doctrines provide great insight into God's future for this planet. Next, Burke says the escapology doctrine ministries employ fear, greed, and extortion to receive tithes by false dictate. He maintains that In That Day Teachings enable believers to hear and obey God, including how much and to whom to give to—with

172

greater emphasis on person-to-person giving. He says, "Bad doctrine creates evil that evil inhabits and expands; while good doctrine creates good that God inhabits and expands." Hence, wishful-thinking doctrines of escape create epic error for its blind leaders and followers. Puerile escape doctrines cause weak praise, wispy voices, and baby-talking pastors and staff who believe their milk-toast messages are the meatiest of steaks. Such pastors throw tantrums if comments are made about the immaturity of themselves and their ill-fed sheep. Enterprises of ease have sold billions of dollars of Christian escapist books, movies, and ministry messages as being nothing but the gospel truth. Escape doctrines also have blinded some prosperity preachers to rather gross adventures in avarice. So, great evil has been called good. Thus, the errant but widely broadcast Christian world view, or Weltanschauung, states Christ's basic *history* correctly but wrongly escapes from Christ's *future*, which forces them to horrifically miss and disbelieve what is happening in Christ's *today*. No message to *escapology* Christians could be more ironic or harder to accept. This message would require escapist leaders to repent of epic misdeeds. And it would require a harlot church to own up to gargantuan logs in its eyes and stupor in its soul caused by easy, infantile doctrines. These In That Day Teachings offer an apostolic Rosetta Stone to see the future better than what the rich salesmen of escape and its sycophants of false hope have left behind. This *tour de force* opus magnum pulls the curtains back on shenanigans in Church, to discover what's wrong, to do right... and thereby discover Jesus offers much, much more.

Above all, a good heaven,
Beneath all, a good foundation,
In all, a good God.

"There are a thousand hacking at the branches of evil to one who is striking at the root."—Henry D. Thoreau